JOURNEY OF *Hope*

JOURNEY OF

Understanding God's Presence in a Broken World

Kathleen M. McGee
Val J. Peter

TEACHER GUIDE

Boys Town, Nebraska

Journey of Hope
Teacher Guide

Published by the Boys Town Press
Boys Town, Nebraska 68010

© 2001 Father Flanagan's Boys' Home

ISBN 1-889322-45-8

All rights reserved. Copying of the student activity worksheets, homework, handouts, and overhead pages of this manual is permitted for classroom purposes only. No other part of this book may be reproduced or transmitted in any form or by any means, electronic or mechanical, including photocopying, recording, or by any information storage and retrieval system, without the written permission of Boys Town Press, except where permitted by law. For information, address Boys Town Press, 14100 Crawford St., Boys Town, NE 68010.

www.girlsandboystown.org/btpress

The Boys Town Press is the publishing division of Girls and Boys Town, the original Father Flanagan's Boys' Home.

All Scripture passages used in this guide are taken from the Holy Bible, Contemporary English Version, copyright, 1999, American Bible Society, New York.

10 9 8 7 6 5 4 3 2 1

JOURNEY OF HOPE

Table of Contents

	Preface	vii
	Acknowledgments	ix
Part One		
	Introduction	1
CHAPTER 1	Getting Started	5
CHAPTER 2	Sample Lesson Plans: Skills for Success	19
Part Two		
SESSION 1	What Is a Prophet?	37
SESSION 2	God Chooses Isaiah	45
SESSION 3	Isaiah's Message	53
SESSION 4	God's Promise of Hope and Healing	61
SESSION 5	God Calls Jeremiah	63
SESSION 6	Jeremiah's Messages	75

SESSION 7	Jeremiah: The New Covenant	83
SESSION 8	Lamentations: Handling Hardships	93
SESSION 9	God Calls Ezekial	101
SESSION 10	Ezekial's Warnings	107
SESSION 11	Ezekial's Messages of Hope	113
SESSION 12	Hosea	123
SESSION 13	Hosea: God's Love Is 'Hessed'	129
SESSION 14	Amos: Do the Right Thing	135
SESSION 15	Malachi: Respect Me by What You Do	145
SESSION 16	Malachi: Worship God Sincerely	161
SESSION 17	Jonah: Prophetic Parable about God's Forgiveness	171
SESSION 18	Jonah: Sin, Consequences, and Repentance	187
SESSION 19	The Sign of Jonah	197
SESSION 20	Micah: Do Justice, Be Merciful, Humbly Obey God	203
SESSION 21	Joel: Repent, Restore, Reveal	219
	Appendix: Social Skills	231

JOURNEY OF HOPE

Preface

Much has been written recently about the process of globalization in the increasingly divided world of the haves and the have-nots. Much less has been written about the youth of the world today who are also divided, but in a different way.

There is a group of youth all over the world, rather small in numbers, who are tuned into the global scene via the Internet, satellites, and e-mail. In China, America, Russia, Kosovo, and elsewhere, you see them promoting a social vision of human rights and personal freedoms, accountable leaderships and economic opportunity not part of a nationalist indoctrination, but a global message of values shared with activists in so many countries. These youth have courage when their elders keep silent.

There is a much larger group of youth today who are living a social vision of hopelessness, alienation, lack of close family ties, and anger against the adult world. These kids are the lonely ones. The loneliness is not of their own making. It is a social phenomenon where families are fractured, where societies couldn't care less, and where kids are considered an economic factor for exploitation via drugs, alcohol, and sex by whomever has the strongest message.

Both of these groups – different as they are – have one thing in common: They do not know that God put them on this earth for a purpose, for a mission. The discovery of this purpose and the embracing of this mission will bring a positive energy into their lives that they could not dream of now. There is an old phrase in the civil rights movement: "If you lose your purpose, you lose your power."

The *Journey of Hope* is meant to help these young people find and cling to the hope they very much need in their lives. This is one of the most powerful courses that young people can possibly encounter. Please use it joyfully, energetically, and feel free to make mid-course corrections as you go along.

Journey of Hope is not meant to be a Catechism. It is meant to be an ecumenical supplement to Catechetical materials of all Christian denominations – a jumpstart that will help young people move with joy and enthusiasm into Catechetical sources.

We here at the Center for Adolescent and Family Spirituality have used this course with great, great success with many, many young people. All the best to you.

>VAL J. PETER
>Executive Director
>Girls and Boys Town

JOURNEY OF HOPE

Acknowledgments

A very special thanks to the following people who contributed in so many ways to the *Journey of Hope* curriculum:

Fr. Val J. Peter, Executive Director, Girls and Boys Town, a master teacher and theologian, for giving shape and form to the content of this curriculum; for sharing his wisdom, experience, and expertise; and for his consistent loving guidance.

The Boys Town High School Religion Teachers for teaching and refining this curriculum; for their insights and feedback, and, most of all, for sharing God's love with our students:

Don L. Bader	Pastor Charles Smith
Fr. Eugene McReynolds	Yvonne Wilson
Sandra Stovall	Mike Petry

Jane Fry, Administrative Assistant, for her organizational and word processing skills, and her patient endurance during all the editorial revisions.

Barbara Lonnborg and the staff of the Boys Town Press for layout, cover design, and production assistance.

JOURNEY OF HOPE

Introduction

The Journey Continues

Sin, evil, apathy, hardship, and temptation – all these plague us today as surely as they did people in the times of the Old Testament. Where do we find the strength to battle these afflictions? How can we be sure of forgiveness if we sin?

Journey of Hope is a religious education curriculum designed to help youth answer these difficult questions from a faith-based perspective. In this curriculum, they study the lives and words of the Biblical Prophets. Through the eyes of the Prophets, they witness the consequences of sinfulness and unwillingness to repent. They also hear how God's love and mercy can restore and redeem those who abandon sin and follow the Commandments.

After reading and discussing the stories of the Prophets, students are challenged to apply what they have learned to how they can handle the sin, temptations, and hardships they face in their own life's journey. *Journey of Hope* brings God's message of hope and restoration to teens at a critical time in their lives – as they begin to make the decisions that will determine who they will become.

Journey of Hope can be used on its own or can be used as a follow-up to the *Journey of Faith* curriculum.

Structure of Each Session

Each session is structured to provide both the learner and the teacher a balanced and comprehensive approach to the subject matter. The religious education methodology employed is a blend of theory and practice that has proven successful with teens in both classroom and youth group settings.

The methodology for each session will usually include each of the following steps:

PRAYER – Sets the tone for the session and reminds us who we are and why we are gathered. One tried and true method for involving youth in leading and participating in opening prayer is the ACTS model prayer. See pages 23-27 for how to teach and employ the ACTS model prayer with your youth.

REVIEW – This enables students to connect topics from previous sessions to the current session. It also serves as a time to review and expand on homework topics.

OBJECTIVE – Introduces learners to the session by briefly explaining the goal of the session.

ACTIVITY – Students participate in a learning activity designed to make the session's objective come alive.

CONNECTION – At this point in the lesson, the teacher will begin to help students make connections between the learning activity and the religious content of the session. This often involves a scripted mini-lecture by the teacher that is copied as notes by the students.

REFLECTION – Students are given reflection questions designed to help them apply the religious content of this session to their own lives.

ACTION – A homework assignment designed to engage students in continued learning on the topic.

Journey of Hope Reader

The *Journey of Hope Reader* is a compilation of inspirational stories, poems, and prayers designed for use as complementary reading and reflection. Each chapter of the reader is based on themes and topics from the sessions in the *Journey of Hope* curriculum. For easy reference, the corresponding Reader chapter is noted at the beginning of each session plan.

The Reader can be used in a variety of ways:

- For homework assignments
- As a class, students can read and discuss the chapter(s) noted before or after the actual session
- As extra credit reading and reflection
- As a class, students can read and reflect on one inspirational story every day as the opening prayer

JOURNEY OF HOPE
CHAPTER 1

Getting Started

Building Relationships

When thinking of how to best build good relationships with the youth in your classroom or group, think of Jesus, our Master Teacher. Jesus knew He had only a short time to teach his twelve disciples all they needed to know. But He didn't just set up a classroom, order books, and prepare outlines.

Jesus invited those twelve, and many others, to live, work, and walk with Him. He invited them into relationship with Him. And it was in the midst of living and relating that the disciples learned the most.

We want students to learn how to have genuine, positive, affirming Christian relationships – with peers and with adults. One of our tasks then is to model and build good relationships.

Here are some things you can do to model and build good relationships:

- Really listen to the youth – individually and as a group.
- Show genuine interest in their lives and stories.
- Be encouraging and supportive.
- Pay attention to discover their gifts and talents.

- Invite them to use their gifts and talents in ministry – in the congregation and in the community.
- Look for something they do well and affirm it.
- Give sincere compliments.
- Say "thanks" for their time, their help, their ideas, their enthusiasm, and so forth.
- Use your sense of humor – but never be sarcastic.
- Do not speak ill of someone; those who hear will wonder what you will say about them.
- Practice and enforce the Golden Rule.
- Talk a little about your own life and spiritual journey (as appropriate).
- Stay in touch in between meetings by attending school or social events or writing a note of thanks or praise.

Many of these relationship-building blocks are ones your youth can use as well. Model the behaviors, teach skills, encourage their use, and affirm youth as they practice building good relationships.

Following the Jesus Way, you and your youth will create a safe and welcoming atmosphere where both relationships and learning will flourish.

Setting Boundaries

Another very important component of creating and maintaining good relationships is setting and maintaining appropriate boundaries for the youth in your class. Setting and maintaining boundaries helps create a positive and safe learning environment.

Such an environment helps foster spiritual growth in youth.

What Is a Boundary?

- A boundary is a limit for behaviors.
- A boundary is a rule or guideline.
- A boundary is a standard; a specific description of what is expected and what is appropriate.

Some examples of boundaries are:

> *"One person speaks at a time."*
>
> *"Keep your hands to yourself."*
>
> *"Be on time."*
>
> *"Use appropriate language. No cussing or swear words."*
>
> *"Show respect for others by not putting them down."*

Why Do Youth Need Boundaries?

We all need to know the limits; what is acceptable behavior, what to do and not to do. Established and enforced boundaries help youth recognize the limits and enable them to take more personal responsibility for their actions.

Boundaries keep us safe, emotionally and physically. They help us learn how to show respect for others, and in the process, help us feel better about ourselves. Establishing and reinforcing boundaries help to create an environment where youth can feel comfortable enough to share faith and safe enough to open themselves more to God's love and grace.

Without boundaries, there are no clear limits for behaviors. When what is expected and appropriate is left unsaid or is unclear, we set youth up to fail. Youth are much more likely to rise to the challenge and engage in respectful behaviors if boundaries are clearly stated and reinforced up front.

Types of Boundaries

Physical Boundaries – enable us to protect and honor our bodies as the "Temple of the Holy Spirit." (Romans 8)

We are not only responsible for the spiritual well-being of the youth we work with, but also for their physical well-being. It is always important to give kids clear and specific instructions and rules. Whether in a classroom, on a youth group trip, at a community service project, or on a retreat, adults need to create and maintain a safe environment for youth.

Emotional/Spiritual Boundaries – enable us to protect personal thoughts, feelings, and experiences.

We undertake the awesome task of helping youth grow spiritually. One way to help foster spiritual growth is to create and maintain a welcoming atmosphere. Sprucing up your actual meeting place can help, but it's even more effective to set and maintain specific expectations and rules for how to treat one another. Spiritual growth involves building good relationships with God and others, sharing one's faith, self-disclosing, asking questions, and praying. Each of these activities involves risking and trusting. Our task is to create and maintain an environment with clear boundaries so that youth can be assured that they will be respected, listened to, and cared for, no matter what.

When to Set Boundaries

The most effective time to set boundaries is at the beginning of the year, or at the first session of your planned meetings. Once established, list and post these boundaries so they can be referred to often. It can be helpful to remind youth of these boundaries:

- After holiday or vacation time
- Before an upcoming event – to proactively teach specific boundaries
- After a problem has occurred – in order to correct inappropriate behavior and remind them of boundaries and why we follow them

Who Establishes the Boundaries?

The principal, religious education director, and teachers, along with parents and adults from your community, should give specific input as to what behaviors are expected and appropriate for youth. Along with clarifying what is expected from youth, these adults should also establish guidelines for what to do when boundaries are broken. It may be helpful to include selected youth leaders from your congregation or school to be a part of this initial conversation. These youth may be able to provide insights and situational examples that can help determine more clear, fair, and necessary recommendations.

After you have clear ideas and direction from adults and parents, the next step is to meet with the youth themselves. Try the following activity to help youth name, clarify, and take ownership of specific boundaries they will need to follow to create and maintain a caring Christian environment.

Step 1. Ask the youth to brainstorm and list their responses to these two questions:

- What damages or destroys our relationships with God and/or others?
- What builds or nourishes our relationships with God and/or others?

Encourage youth to name specific actions and attitudes that fit into each list. (Damages – rumors, cheating, two-faced behavior, talking behind one's back. Nourishes – respect, spending time, listening, etc.) Allow students plenty of time to add to the list. Make sure adults wait to add to either list until youth have finished.

Step 2. Discuss and compare their lists.

Again, allow plenty of time for their responses. Hopefully, they will notice that the contents of these two lists are usually opposites of one another. They may also notice that contents of these lists are:

- how we want to be treated or don't want to be treated by others.
- very similar to two important religious teachings – the Golden Rule and the Ten Commandments.

Post a list of the Ten Commandments next to their lists from Step 1. Ask students to name any similarities between their lists and the Ten Commandments. They will notice, that in some way or another, most or all of the Ten Commandments are represented in their lists. You as teacher may need to point out some of the similarities or make some generalizations between their lists and the Ten Commandments. For example, your students may not list "killing or murdering someone" as something that destroys or damages relationships. However, most teens will usually list something like spreading gossip or destroying someone's reputation. Gossip or destruction of someone's reputation may not physically harm another person, but it can emotionally and spiritually damage another person, and in this sense, is breaking that commandment.

Finally, point out that some people today say that the Ten Commandments are outdated, old-fashioned, or not applicable to today's world. But, as they just named many of them on their lists, the behaviors and boundaries reflected in the Ten Commandments are still important to us today. This activity reminds students that God's law is written on our hearts – we know it and can name it as how we want and don't want to be treated by others. The Ten Commandments are one way God teaches us how to have healthy and nourishing relationships with Him and with one another.

Step 3. Next, explain to the students the purpose of this activity:

"This activity was designed to help us begin to think about the specific boundaries we need to keep in this classroom/youth group in order to create a truly Christian environment where relationships are nourished, not damaged. You have just listed how you want and don't want to be treated by others and you've reviewed how God calls us to treat one another as named in His Ten Commandments. Let's now create our own list of the Ten Most Important Boundaries/Rules for Behavior for our class time/meeting time."

Before naming boundaries, offer youth these helpful suggestions:

1. **Keep it simple.** State the boundary clearly and concisely.

    "One person speaks at a time."

    "Disagree appropriately."

2. **State it positively.** Tell them what they should do and how to do it.

    "Thou SHALL..." instead of *"Thou shall NOT..."*

    "Be in the classroom, at your desk, before the bell rings."

3. **Adhere to the "Golden Rule."** Always keep in mind how you want/deserve to be treated as a child of God.

When the students are finished listing their ideas, add any other boundaries you deem necessary.

Step 4. Create and post your new list of boundaries alongside a poster naming the Ten Commandments.

Send copies home to parents to read and discuss. Refer to these lists often!

Step 5: MAKE SURE to let kids know that these boundaries are EXPECTATIONS.

Let them know that if they break a boundary, there will be consistent consequences and explain what those consequences will be. Be sure to consult with your principal, director of religious education, or pastor for exact procedures regarding consequences. It is most important that the youth know that:

1. There are specific boundaries for behaviors that everyone is expected to follow.

2. Maintaining these boundaries will help make a Christian environment where all are safe and welcomed.

3. There are pre-established and appropriate consequences for breaking boundaries. (More on how to set and enforce consequences later)

4. The teacher or another designated adult will address any broken boundaries in a fair and dignified way. (More on this in the next section)

Be sure to explain why it is important for all of us to maintain appropriate and healthy boundaries.

- *"They help us know how to treat one another and how we can expect to be treated."*

- *"Following these rules will help us all learn to show respect to others."*

- *"Maintaining boundaries helps us create good Christian relationships."*

Methods for Maintaining Boundaries

Along with naming boundaries, you also need to know ways to maintain and reinforce boundaries with youth. Following are three tried and true methods from the Youth Care Specialists at Girls and Boys Town.

Proactive Teaching

Set youth up for success by specifically naming and briefly explaining the boundaries/expected behaviors before each event/activity. A little preventive teaching goes a long way in stopping inappropriate behaviors before they get started.

The steps to Proactive Teaching are:

Step 1. Describe the behaviors that are appropriate and/or expected for this event/activity.

Step 2. Give a reason.

Step 3. Practice. (optional)

Example – In a Girls Support Group, gossiping and complaining can quickly ruin a good discussion. Use Proactive Teaching to remind the girls:

a) *"When describing a problem or situation, please do not use any names. Stick to talking only about yourself and your feelings. No blaming or complaining."*

b) *"It's important to do this for many reasons: Because no one wants to be talked about behind his or her back; it is not fair to discuss someone who is not present; we are about solving problems, not laying blame or complaining."*

It's amazing how these simple boundaries can prevent potentially serious problems and enable students to speak more freely, trust one another more, and resolve conflicts in a more responsible fashion!

Effective Praise

One of the best ways to help youth do the right thing in the future is to "catch them doing the right thing." We all need reassurance that we're doing what we are supposed to. We all like to receive praise and compliments. A great way to ensure that a positive behavior is repeated is to recognize it with praise. Tell youth when they're doing a good job, and be sure to name exactly what it is that they are doing right. Then they'll know exactly what to do the next time!

The steps to Effective Praise are:

Step 1. Show your approval. Smile, speak a word of praise or thanks, or give a pat on the back.

Step 2. Describe the positive. Name it specifically: *"Alan, thanks for waiting for Juana to finish speaking before stating your point."* or, *"Allison, I really appreciated your note to let me know that you'd be late for the planning meeting!"*

Step 3. Give a reason. Tell them why what they did was good, important, or helpful. To Alan: *"Waiting for someone to finish speaking before you speak is a great way to show respect and to show that you are really listening!"* To Allison: *"Your note helped me use that extra time wisely instead of worrying and waiting."*

Corrective Teaching

Boundary breaking is "bound" to happen. We all cross a boundary now and then, sometimes by accident and sometimes on purpose. Our task as adults is to provide consistent management of boundaries, whether kept or broken. It is important to know, in advance, what to do when boundaries/rules are broken. Corrective Teaching, another proven method from the Youth Care Specialists at Girls and Boys Town, coupled with appropriate consequences, is a most effective method for transforming a broken boundary into a teachable moment.

The steps to Corrective Teaching are:

Step 1. Stop the problem behavior. As soon as you notice a broken boundary, address it. Sometimes just moving closer to the problem behavior – moving to sit next to two whispering teens, or catching the eye of those involved – can stop the problem. Other times a prompt, spoken in a calm and descriptive manner, can help kids get back on track: *"Remember, no talking during the Prayer Service."*

Step 2. Give a consequence. Sometimes it is enough of a consequence to have an adult leader or teacher sit next to the student or to be gently prompted in front of the whole group. Other times, a more substantial consequence is needed.

Following are some guidelines for consequences:

- **Consequences should be established by adults and communicated to youth and parents in advance!** Don't wait for a situation to arise before deciding what the consequence will be. It is best to have predetermined consequences that are well communicated to all before any boundaries are broken. Consequences decided on the spur of the moment can too easily become punishing, vengeful, or too drastic.

- **Consequences should never be degrading or humiliating.** They should be opportunities for learning responsibility.

- **Consequences should be given fairly and consistently.** All youth should be held accountable for maintaining these boundaries. Don't play favorites or let youth talk their way out of owning up to their behavior.

- **Corrective Teaching and consequences should be done one-to-one whenever possible,** even if it means taking a youth aside for a moment. It is rarely effective to correct a youth in front of a group. Usually this causes anger and embarrassment, and you run the risk of escalating the problem rather than correcting it.

- **Ask for help from parents and other adults.** Sometimes the presence of other parents or adults helps youth stay on track. These "extra" adults could be used as "time-out" folks – someone to send a youth to be with if his or her behavior causes the youth to be removed from the large group activity. The "time-out" folks are not meant to be disciplinarians, but rather an option for a youth who may need some extra one-on-one time.

Step 3. Describe the positive behavior the youth should do. Now that the youth knows what not to do, let him or her know what to do: *"Instead of whispering to Shannon, please give your quiet attention to our guest speaker."*

Step 4. Give youth a chance to engage in positive behavior. Now is your chance to back away and allow the youth to turn his or her behavior around. Watch for any steps in the right direction and give praise for it. Again, most of this can be done in low voice tones, one on one, without disturbing or calling attention from the rest of the group, although there may be times when you have to stop the group activity and address a major boundary breaking.

Addressing and correcting any problems promptly and without much disruption sends a powerful message to the whole group. It lets them know that you are watching out for them, that you care about how they treat one another, and that you keep your word. They need to see that you will be firm, yet gentle, in safeguarding their boundaries. Your actions speak much louder than words in these instances.

Always remember the Golden Rule when correcting behaviors: Treat a youth as you would want to be treated. Put yourself in that teen's place. Show genuine empathy and understanding rather than anger or domination. When dealing with difficult situations, remember these two adages:

"A gentle response turns away wrath."

"Love the sinner, hate the sin!"

Top Ten Boundaries for Youth Group Activities

Here are some time-tested, success-inspiring, "catch 'em being good" boundaries that address areas of behavior that are common to most religious education settings.

1. **One person speaks at a time.** Whether in small or large group discussions, this is an ever-present opportunity to show respect and to really listen to what everyone has to say.

2. **Disagree appropriately.** This is a very important skill to teach, model, role-play, and use. Disagreeing appropriately allows opinions to be voiced without aggression or disrespect. It teaches us how to accept and allow others to be different. It can defuse tense situations. (See the next section for more about this skill and others.)

3. **No putdowns allowed.** Show respect to others by refraining from making value judgments about them: *"You may not use words like 'stupid,' 'dumb,' 'ugly,' 'gross,' or other judgmental, negative words to describe people or their thoughts. Say 'please be quiet' instead of 'shut up.' No teasing, even if only in fun."*

4. **Say whatever you want as long as it is appropriate** – as long as what is said is on the topic and does not contain any obscene or offensive language.

5. **What is said here, stays here** – except for when an adult needs to seek help for a teen in danger. When anyone makes any reference to doing something harmful or illegal to himself or herself or someone else, we need to speak up and seek help. Do not keep this information to yourself. This boundary helps create trust, safety, and a sense of community.

6. **Self-disclose appropriately.** Personal dumping, public confessions, blaming or complaining are never allowed. If any of these happen, the teacher should politely interrupt and steer the conversation back on track.

7. **Practice good listening skills.** Looking at the person who is speaking, concentrating on what is being said, etc., all show respect and value of others.

8. **Observe school/church rules about public displays of affection (PDA).** Yes, it is important to state this clearly. Public displays of affection can cause serious problems among youth groups. Some recommended PDA rules: "Refrain from hand holding, kissing, cuddling, or any other form of exclusive affection at school/church activities; ask permission before giving a hug – especially to newcomers."

9. **Ask for help** – from adults or youth leaders whenever you need it.

10. **Participate.** *"You get out of class what you put into class. So get into it!"*

Boundaries for One-to-Ones with Teens

When a teen asks to talk to you privately, there are some important boundaries to make known:

1. **Some things cannot be kept secret.** Let teens know that if they share thoughts of hurting themselves or someone else, or reveal involvement in illegal, sexual, or abusive activity, that you have a moral obligation to tell someone else who can help them. In these serious circumstances, a teen's physical, emotional, and spiritual life is at stake. We must let kids know that we value their life above all else, even above their possible anger at "telling" on them.

2. **Meet in an open space where you can be seen, but not overheard, by others.** If meeting in an office, keep the door open, or use only an office with uncovered windows. This can prevent any allegations of misconduct and provide you both with the security of knowing others are around.

3. **Remind kids that you are not a trained counselor, but that you can point them in the right direction.** Have referral sources available with names and phone numbers of professionals who can help.

Skills That Build Boundaries and Help Prevent Conflict

The best way to resolve a conflict is to prevent it! We can help prevent some conflict by teaching, practicing, and modeling good social skills. What is a skill? It is a step-by-step approach, a "how to" method, of demonstrating proper social behaviors.

Many conflicts arise because of inappropriate or misunderstood verbal or non-verbal communications. Learning more about and practicing social skills can help youth learn how to relate to one another and to adults in a more appropriate and Christian fashion. Here are some examples:

- How to disagree appropriately
- How to accept criticism
- How to give/accept compliments
- How to ask for help
- How to share personal experiences
- How to express empathy and understanding for others
- How to follow instructions
- How to apologize/accept apologies

The steps to these skills can be found in the Appendix.

JOURNEY OF HOPE
CHAPTER 2

Sample Lesson Plans: Skills for Success

The following are samples of actual lesson plans used by Catholic and Protestant religion teachers at Boys Town High School at the beginning of each semester. Each lesson is designed to help youth master certain skills or obtain information that will be helpful throughout the semester. Of special interest is Lesson Plan 2: How to Pray. The lesson introduces the ACTS model of prayer, used daily as the opening prayer in each high school class.

LESSON PLAN 1: Boundaries for Successful Relationships

LESSON PLAN 2: How to Pray – Participating and Leading Class in Prayer

LESSON PLAN 3: How to Locate Passages in the Bible

LESSON PLAN 4: Building Community in the Classroom

LESSON PLAN 1: Boundaries for Successful Relationships

OBJECTIVE

To introduce and explain classroom rules and behavior expectations.

PREPARATION

Have ready for use:
- Markers, chalk
- Blank poster board, paper, or chalkboard
- Poster-size copy of the Ten Commandments

PRAYER

Opening prayer

OBJECTIVE

State objective as described at left.

ACTIVITY

1. Draw two columns on the chalkboard or poster paper. Write at the top of one of the columns: "Behaviors or attitudes that damage or destroy relationships with God and/or others." Title the other column: "Behaviors or attitudes that build or nourish relationships with God and/or others."

2. Next, ask students to brainstorm and name specific behaviors or attitudes that belong in each column. Encourage students to be as specific as possible. For example, if a student says, "Disrespect damages relationships," affirm her response and then ask her to be more specific by saying, *"Tell me what disrespect sounds like or looks like? How do you know if someone is being disrespectful you?"* This technique enables students to describe more clearly the behaviors and attitudes they find disrespectful.

CONNECTION

1. Once their lists are complete, ask the students, *"What do you notice about these lists?"* Allow for a variety of responses. Make sure to point out that what they have named is how each of them wants or does not want to be treated by others, also known as the Golden Rule.

2. Next, post a list of the Ten Commandments beside their lists. Ask: *"What similarities do you notice between your lists and God's Ten Commandments?"* Allow for various responses. Usually, they will notice that in some way or another most, if not all, of the Ten Commandments are somehow named in their lists. As

the teacher, you may need to point out some of the connections that they might miss. For example, your students may not name "murder" (the 5th Commandment) as a behavior that destroys relationships, but most teens will usually name gossiping or ruining someone's reputation as behavior that damages relationships. Though gossiping does no physical harm, it certainly can cause emotional or spiritual damage to another and in this way breaks that commandment.

3. Finally, point out that some people today say that the Ten Commandments are outdated, old-fashioned, or not applicable to today's world. But, as they just noticed, the behaviors and boundaries reflected in the Ten Commandments are still important to us today. This activity should remind students that God's law is written on our hearts – we know it and can name it as how we want and don't want to be treated by others. The Ten Commandments are one way God is trying to teach us how to have healthy and nourishing relationships with Him and with one another.

REFLECTION

Explain: *"This activity was designed to help us begin to think about the specific boundaries we need to keep in this classroom/youth group in order to create a truly Christian environment where relationships are nourished, not damaged. You have just listed how you want and don't want to be treated by others, and you've reviewed how God calls us to treat one another as named in His Ten Commandments. Let's now create our own list of the Ten Most Important Boundaries/Rules for Behavior for our class time/meeting time."*

Before naming boundaries, offer youth these helpful suggestions:

1. Keep it simple. State the boundary clearly and concisely.

    "One person speaks at a time."

    "Disagree appropriately."

2. State it positively. Name what should be done and how to do it. *"Thou SHALL..."* instead of *"Thou shall NOT..."*

   "Be in the classroom, at your desk, before the bell rings."

3. Adhere to the "Golden Rule." Always keep in mind how you want/deserve to be treated as a child of God.

When the students are finished listing their ideas, add any other boundaries you deem necessary.

ACTION

Post the new class list of boundaries alongside a poster naming the Ten Commandments.

Send copies home to parents to read and discuss. When in class/youth group refer to these lists often!

MAKE SURE students know that these boundaries are EXPECTATIONS for classroom/youth group behavior. Let them know that if they break a boundary, there will be consistent consequences and explain what those consequences will be. Be sure to consult with your principal, director of religious education, or pastor for exact procedures regarding consequences. It is most important that the youth know that:

- There are specific boundaries for behaviors that everyone is expected to follow.
- Maintaining these boundaries will help make this a Christian environment where all are safe and welcomed.
- There are pre-established and appropriate consequences for breaking boundaries.
- The teacher or another designated adult will address any broken boundaries in a fair and dignified way.

Be sure to explain why it is important for all of us to maintain appropriate and healthy boundaries.

- *"They help us know how to treat one another and how we can expect to be treated."*

- *"Following these rules will help us all learn to show respect to others."*
- *"Maintaining boundaries helps us create good Christian relationships."*

LESSON PLAN 2: How to Pray – Participating and Leading Class in Prayer

PRAYER
Ask for a volunteer to read Scripture and lead prayer.

OBJECTIVE
State objective as described at right.

REVIEW
Ask if anyone knows what the components of the ACTS model prayer stand for (A – Adoration or praise, C – Confession, T – Thanksgiving, S – Supplication).

ACTIVITY

1. Show Overhead 1. Briefly explain each component of the ACTS model while students take notes. Explain by saying: *"The ACTS model is one way of praying or communicating with God."* It has four components:

    A – The first component is A, which stands for **Adoration**. It means to praise God for something that He is.

    C – The C stands for **Confession**. It means to admit to God our wrongdoings.

    T – Stands for **Thanksgiving**. In this component we thank God for what He has done for us or given us.

    S – Stands for **Supplication**. This means "to ask for what is needed." In this part of the prayer, we ask God for what we truly need to live good Christian lives.

OBJECTIVE
To introduce and/or review ACTS model of prayer

PREPARATION
Overheads for this session, student handouts

2. Next lead the class in brainstorming examples of each component of the ACTS model. On a blank overhead transparency or the chalkboard, write "A – Adoration/praise." List their ideas for what we could praise or adore God for being (*We praise You God for being... Father, Friend, Leader, Helper, Forgiver, etc.*). Do the same for C – Confession, T – Thanksgiving, and S – Supplication. (Examples for each could include: *"We confess that we... sin, hurt ourselves and others, do not always follow your ways, are sometimes selfish, etc. We thank You God for... life, health, food, shelter, love, etc. We ask You God for... healing, hope, strength, peace, etc."*)

3. After brainstorming, have students copy these examples and keep them. They can use them as a reference for future prayer writing.

CONNECTION

Now go back to each component and give rationales for why each one is an important part of praying. Give rationales for why we praise God, why we thank God, why we confess to God, and why and what we ask God for. You could have students take notes on this as well.

REFLECTION

Show overhead of blank ACTS model prayer form and have class compose a group ACTS model prayer for practice. Then have students individually practice writing ACTS prayers of their own. Teacher should circulate to check writing and give ideas/feedback.

ACTION

Once all prayers are completed, have students hand them in to be checked. Homework assignment could be to write three more ACTS model prayers of their own.

Distribute the student handout, "How to Lead Prayer," and review it with the class. Instruct students to keep this handout accessible for reference when leading class prayer.

LESSON 2 — HOW TO PRAY
OVERHEAD 1

ACTS Model Prayer

A -

C -

T -

S -

LESSON 2 — HOW TO PRAY
OVERHEAD 2

DEAR GOD,

    A   We praise You, God, for being...

    C   We confess that...

    T   We thank You for...

    S   We ask You...

In Your Son's name, we pray, Amen.

© 2001 by Father Flanagan's Boys' Home.

JOURNEY OF HOPE

LESSON 2 HOW TO PRAY
STUDENT HANDOUT

How to Lead Prayer

Step 1. Scripture

A. Look up Scripture passage posted on board.

B. Decide if you want to read Scripture aloud or ask another student to read for you.

C. Wait for teacher's instructions to begin.

D. (In Catholic groups, lead class in the sign of the Cross.)

E. Read Scripture slowly and clearly.

Step 2. ACTS Model Prayer

A. Use ACTS model to say a prayer.

B. Begin by saying:

Dear God,

We praise You for being...

We confess that...

We thank You for...

We ask You...

In Your Son's name, we pray, Amen.

C. Ask "Are there any special intentions?" and allow classmates time to say their prayer intentions aloud.

Step 3. Closing Prayer

A. Decide which prayer to lead (The Hail Mary, The Lord's Prayer, The Glory Be, etc.)

B. Say "Please join me in saying the Lord's Prayer" (or whichever prayer you choose). Then lead class in that prayer.

C. Say "AMEN." (Lead Catholic class in the Sign of the Cross to close prayer.)

© 2001 by Father Flanagan's Boys' Home.

JOURNEY OF HOPE

LESSON PLAN 3: How to Locate Passages in the Bible

OBJECTIVE

To review and/or learn how to find passages in the Bible using Title, Chapter, and Verse

PREPARATION

- Bible for each student
- Student handouts for this session
- Copies of pages of the Bible to use with Activity worksheet
- Overheads for this session
- Overheads of photocopied pages from the Bible
- Yellow, green, red markers for students

PRAYER

Ask for a volunteer to read Scripture and lead class in ACTS prayer.

REVIEW

Review the previous session by asking:

"What are the components of the ACTS model prayer?"

"Why do we Praise God, Thank God, Confess to God, and Ask God for our needs?"

OBJECTIVE

State objective as described at left.

ACTIVITY

Give a five-minute mini-lecture on a few important facts about the Bible. (Use Overhead 1 for basis of lecture). Have students copy these as notes about the Bible to be kept in their class folder or notebook.

CONNECTION

1. Say: *"Now that you know a few facts about the Bible, let's learn (or review) how to find passages in the Bible using Title, Chapter, and Verse."*

2. Have a Scripture passage written on the board, for example, Matthew 13: 7-9. Ask if anyone knows which is the title, which is the chapter, and which is the verse. After students have responded, point out: *"The name of the passage, or the book of the Bible from which the passage is taken is called the Title. The number that follows the title is called the Chapter number. The numbers that follow the Chapter number are called the Verse numbers. Verse numbers are the small numbers you see within the paragraphs of the written text of the Bible."*

3. Show Overhead 2 and use for guided group practice. Point to a particular title, chapter, or verse and ask for volunteers to identify it. Make sure all students are called upon sometime during practice.

4. Show overheads of photocopied pages from the Bible. (You'll need to create your own overheads for this activity.) Invite volunteers to come forward and point to a particular title, chapter number, or verse number of your choosing.

REFLECTION

Next distribute Activity worksheet for this session for students to complete as individual practice. They should hand it in when completed.

ACTION

Distribute Homework worksheet, "Locating Bible Passages."

LESSON 3 HOW TO LOCATE PASSAGES IN THE BIBLE
OVERHEAD 1

A Few Facts About the Bible

1. The Bible is a collection of books written by many different authors over thousands of years.

2. Each author of each book of the Bible was inspired by God to write. Each book tells a piece of the story of how God has been in relationship with His people and how people have looked for, struggled with, and related to God throughout history.

3. The Bible is divided into two main sections – the Old Testament and the New Testament. The Old Testament contains 39 different books. The Catholic version of the Bible adds a few books to the Old Testament. These books are called the Deuterocanonicals/Apocrypha. The Apocrypha was originally included in the earliest versions of the King James Version of the Bible, but its inclusion now is in dispute among some Christians. The New Testament has 27 books.

4. The Old Testament was originally written in Hebrew and Aramaic. It is divided into five sections: the Pentateuch, the Historical Books, Poetic Books, the Major Prophets, and the Minor Prophets. The Old Testament recounts how, over many centuries and through many hardships, God continually loved and called the Hebrew people to be His own.

5. The New Testament was originally written in Greek and divided into four sections: The Gospels and Acts, The Letters of Paul, Other Letters, and Revelation. The New Testament tells the greatest love story of all time – the life, death and resurrection of God's Son, Jesus, and of his disciples, who, by Jesus' instruction and the inspiration of the Holy Spirit, founded and spread the early Christian Church.

LESSON 3: HOW TO LOCATE PASSAGES IN THE BIBLE
OVERHEAD 2

JOHN 3:16

ROMANS 12:1-8

2 CORINTHIANS 2:7-8

LUKE 6:27-31

JEREMIAH 1:4-8

PROVERBS 11:27

1 KINGS 2:1-4

DEUTERONOMY 30:11-18

LESSON 3 — HOW TO LOCATE PASSAGES IN THE BIBLE
ACTIVITY WORKSHEET

Name_____

Locating Bible Passages

Directions: Use the photocopied pages of the Bible stapled to this worksheet when following the instructions below.

Step 1: Go through all the attached photocopied pages from the Bible and circle with a yellow marker every TITLE you can find.

Step 2: Go through all the attached pages from the Bible and underline with a green marker all the CHAPTER NUMBERS you can find.

Step 3: Go through all the attached pages from the Bible and underline in red all the VERSE NUMBERS you can find.

LESSON 3 HOW TO LOCATE PASSAGES IN THE BIBLE
HOMEWORK

Name_____

Locating Bible Passages

Directions: Look up the Scripture passages below. Then fill in the blanks next to each passage.

1. Exodus 20:1-17 is on page_____ in the _____Testament.
   Write out verse number 16:

2. 1 Samuel 24:16-20 is on page_____ in the _____Testament.
   Write out verse number 18:

3. Psalm 63:3-8 is on page_____ in the _____Testament.
   Write out verse number 3:

4. John 13:33-35 is on page_____ in the _____Testament.
   Write out verse number 34:

© 2001 by Father Flanagan's Boys' Home.

JOURNEY OF HOPE

LESSON 3 HOMEWORK – PAGE 2

5. 1 Thessalonians 5:14-22 is on page_____ in the _____Testament.
Write out verse number 17:

6. Galatians 5:22-26 is on page_____ in the _____Testament.
Write out verse number 22:

7. Micah 6:6-8 is on page_____ in the _____Testament.
Write out verse number 8:

8. Jeremiah 1:4-9 is on page_____ in the _____ Testament.
Write out verse number 8:

LESSON PLAN 4: Building Community in the Classroom

PRAYER

Ask for a volunteer to lead prayer or begin assigning daily class prayer leaders. Use Scripture for the day and ACTS model prayer format.

REVIEW

Review facts about Bible or any other previously covered material.

OBJECTIVE

Explain: *"The goal for today's class is to get to know one another better and begin to build positive relationships."*

ACTIVITY

1. Display a picture of a Medieval Coat of Arms. Explain: *"In the Middle Ages, people used to put symbols of themselves and their families on their coat of arms. Sometimes the coat of arms would be on a flag hanging outside their residence or sometimes on a shield carried into battle. Today you're going to create your own personal coat of arms."*

2. Distribute white paper and markers. Draw an outline of a coat of arms on the chalkboard and have students copy it onto their paper. Divide the coat of arms into four or six areas. Label each area one of the following (or something like it):

   - An animal that best symbolizes me
   - A picture that symbolizes something that is important to me
   - Where I hope to live, or what I hope to be doing 10 years from now
   - A slogan or motto that describes my life so far
   - A slogan, motto, or picture that describes my goals for my life

---

OBJECTIVE

To enable students and teacher to build positive relationships that will eventually enhance trust, cooperation, and appropriate sharing in the class.

PREPARATION

- Colored paper
- Markers
- Scissors
- Glue
- Old magazines

- My favorite food
- Something that symbolizes my ethnic/family heritage

Give students plenty of time to draw or cut and paste pictures from magazines to complete their coat of arms.

CONNECTION/REFLECTION

Go around the class and ask each person to explain one or more areas on his or her coat of arms. Use Proactive Teaching to remind students of appropriate behaviors when others are self-disclosing – no putdowns, giving eye contact to speaker, raising hand and waiting to be called on.

ACTION

Possible homework activity – have the students take their coat of arms home and share with a parent.

JOURNEY OF HOPE

SESSION 1

What Is a Prophet?

OBJECTIVE

Enable students to identify the role and characteristics of a prophet.

READER

Chapter 1: What Is a Prophet?

LESSON PLAN

PRAYER

Opening prayer

OBJECTIVE

State as described at left.

ACTIVITY

Show a video segment of Martin Luther King's famous "I Have a Dream" speech, or have a student volunteer read aloud some of the text from this speech. (Other options: show a video segment or have speech text read from other modern day "prophets" such Oscar Romero, Dorothy Day, Billy Graham, or Mother Teresa.) After the video segment or speech, discuss the following:

1. What was the main message of this speech?

2. What do you know about this person?

3. Sometimes this person is called a "modern day prophet." Why do you think that is?

37

4. What is a prophet? How do you become a prophet? What are the characteristics of a prophet?

5. Name other prophets you've heard of.

CONNECTION

Introduce the role and characteristics of a prophet by having students take the following notes:

- A prophet is someone who is called by God, who listens to God, and whose specific purpose in life is to proclaim God's word to the people no matter what the personal cost.

- Prophets spread God's message through both word and deed. (Example: Isaiah going unclothed and barefoot to teach people their need to have eyes and ears of faith.)

- Prophets magnify one point that people are overlooking. Their message is so important that they use obvious exaggerations (hyperbolae) to get the point across powerfully and memorably. You might say prophets have a "one-item agenda" to preach about. (Example: Ezekiel and the Dry Bones)

- Prophets never had it easy. They often lived during times of terrible hardship and often faced rejection and resistance from the people. The Prophets could have given up and done their own selfish will. Instead, they did the will of the Lord.

- There are false prophets and true prophets. How do you know who's who? "By their fruits you shall know them." False prophets tell falsehoods about God and confuse people. True prophets tell what the Lord really wants and eventually their prophecies bring about justice.

- We study the Biblical Prophets today because we can be inspired by:

    their reliable messages of hope and trust in God.

    their commitment to doing God's will no matter what the cost.

    their example of seeking and living out God's purpose for their lives.

REFLECTION

Distribute and explain Reflection Questions worksheet for this session. Complete in class and discuss and/or assign for homework.

ACTION

Have students read Chapter 1 in the *Journey of Hope Reader* for homework.

SESSION 1 — WHAT IS A PROPHET?
ACTIVITY WORKSHEET

Name_____

Reflection Questions

Directions: Review your notes from today's session to help you answer the following questions.

1. List the reasons we study Prophets today.

2. Why do Prophets exaggerate?

3. How do Prophets spread God's message?

4. Describe the times in which many of the Biblical Prophets lived.

5. How did most people react to the Prophets' messages?

SESSION 1 ACTIVITY WORKSHEET – PAGE 2

6. "A Prophet is someone who is _____ by God, who _____ to God, and whose specific purpose in life is to _____.

7. Of the Prophets you've studied so far, whose message applies most to your life? Why?

8. How are you like/unlike a Prophet? Explain.

9. How can you know if someone is a false prophet? Explain.

10. How can you know who a true prophet is? Explain.

SESSION 1 — WHAT IS A PROPHET?
ACTIVITY WORKSHEET

TEACHER'S COPY

Reflection Questions

Directions: Review your notes from today's session to help you answer the following questions.

1. List the reasons we study Prophets today.

   We can be inspired by their messages, their commitment to God, and their life examples.

2. Why do Prophets exaggerate?

   To make their one-item agenda very clear

3. How do Prophets spread God's message?

   By preaching in word and deed

4. Describe the times in which many of the Biblical Prophets lived.

   Usually very troubled times when the Hebrew people were particularly lost, willful, and sinful

5. How did most people react to the Prophets' messages?

   Prophets were usually rejected, harassed, scorned, or ignored.

SESSION 1 ACTIVITY WORKSHEET – PAGE 2   **TEACHER'S COPY**

6. "A Prophet is someone who is _____*called*_____ by God, who _____*listens*_____ to God, and whose specific purpose in life is to _____*preach God's message to the people no matter what the personal cost.*_____.

7. Of the Prophets you've studied so far, whose message applies most to your life? Why?
Open-ended

8. How are you like/unlike a Prophet? Explain.
Open-ended

9. How can you know if someone is a false prophet? Explain.
False prophets preach falsehoods, lies, about God and confuse people.

10. How can you know who a true prophet is? Explain.
True prophets preach God's message and eventually their prophecies bring about justice.

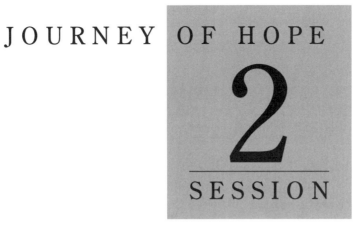

JOURNEY OF HOPE
SESSION 2

God Chooses Isaiah

LESSON PLAN

OBJECTIVE
In this session, students will discover how Isaiah discovered God's purpose for his life.

PREPARATION
Provide Bibles for the students to use in class and for homework. Worksheet answers are based on the Contemporary English Version, American Bible Society, 1999.

READER
Chapter 2: Conscience of a Nation

PRAYER
Opening prayer

REVIEW
Ask students:
1. What is a prophet?
2. Who are some Biblical prophets?
3. Who are some modern-day prophets?

OBJECTIVE
State as described at left.

ACTIVITY
1. Ask for a volunteer to read aloud the introduction to the book of Isaiah as found in the Bible.
2. Next ask for a volunteer to read aloud Isaiah 6:1-8. Use the following questions to discuss this passage

45

and discover more about how Isaiah became a prophet.

a. What role did God call Isaiah to fill?
A prophet

b. How did Isaiah receive God's call?
In a vision

c. Describe Isaiah's vision.

d. What is Isaiah's first response to God's call?
Says no because of his sinfulness – "Every word that passes from my lips is sinful." Feels he is unworthy of God's call.

e. What was God's response to Isaiah's refusal and confession of sin?
God forgives Isaiah and reiterates his choice of Isaiah.

f. What is Isaiah's final response to God's call?
"I will go! Send me to be your messenger!"

CONNECTION

Summarize by having students take the following notes:

- Isaiah was called by God, in a vision, to become a prophet. His purpose was to preach the message about God's holiness to the Hebrew people. Isaiah lived in turbulent times, about 700 years before Jesus.

- At first, Isaiah resisted God's call to be a prophet. When God showed his love through forgiveness, Isaiah was able to accept and accomplish God's purpose for his life.

REFLECTION

Distribute and explain the Reflection Questions worksheet for this session.

ACTION

Distribute and explain Homework worksheet for this session.

SESSION 2 — GOD CHOOSES ISAIAH
ACTIVITY WORKSHEET

Name _____

Reflection Questions

Directions: Re-read Isaiah 6:1-8 and then answer the following reflection questions honestly and seriously.

1. During Isaiah's vision in the temple, he hears the angels say, "Holy, Holy, Holy, The Lord Almighty is Holy. His Glory fills the world." What does it mean to say God is holy?

2. Why do we call God holy?

3. How did Isaiah experience the holiness of God?

4. Why did Isaiah feel he was unworthy of God's call to be a prophet?

© 2001 by Father Flanagan's Boys' Home.

JOURNEY OF HOPE

SESSION 2 ACTIVITY WORKSHEET – PAGE 2

5. How do you think Isaiah felt about receiving forgiveness from God? Why?

6. Describe a time when you received God's forgiveness.

7. How would you respond if God asked you to be His messenger? Explain.

8. What message is God calling you to speak?

9. How have you experienced, or how would you describe, the holiness of God?

SESSION 2 — GOD CHOOSES ISAIAH
ACTIVITY WORKSHEET

TEACHER'S COPY

Reflection Questions

Directions: Re-read Isaiah 6:1-8 and then answer the following reflection questions honestly and seriously.

1. During Isaiah's vision in the temple, he hears the angels say, "Holy, Holy, Holy, The Lord Almighty is Holy. His Glory fills the world." What does it mean to say God is holy?

   Holy means that God is spiritually pure and perfect, deserving our deep respect, reverence, and adoration.

2. Why do we call God holy?

   To remind us who God is and who we are; to praise Him

3. How did Isaiah experience the holiness of God?

   Isaiah experiences God's holiness in his calling, in God's forgiveness, and in receiving from God the ability to preach.

4. Why did Isaiah feel he was unworthy of God's call to be a prophet?

   Because he was sinful

SESSION 2 ACTIVITY WORKSHEET – PAGE 2 **TEACHER'S COPY**

5. How do you think Isaiah felt about receiving forgiveness from God? Why?
Open-ended

6. Describe a time when you received God's forgiveness.
Open-ended

7. How would you respond if God asked you to be His messenger? Explain.
Open-ended

8. What message is God calling you to speak?
Open-ended

9. How have you experienced, or how would you describe, the holiness of God?
Open-ended

SESSION 2: GOD CHOOSES ISAIAH
HOMEWORK

Name_____

Directions: Read the following passages to discover more about one of Isaiah's most important prophecies.

1. Read Isaiah 7:10-25.

   a. Who is Isaiah prophesying about?

   b. How do you know?

2. Read Isaiah 11:1-9.

   a. Who is Isaiah describing in this passage?

   b. How do you know?

3. Read Isaiah 42:1-9.

   a. Who is this passage about?

   b. How do you know?

4. Read Isaiah 53:2-12.

   a. Who is Isaiah describing in this passage?

   b. How do you know?

GOD CHOOSES ISAIAH
HOMEWORK

TEACHER'S COPY

Directions: Read the following passages to discover more about one of Isaiah's most important prophecies.

1. Read Isaiah 7:10-25.

   a. Who is Isaiah prophesying about?

   Jesus

   b. How do you know?

   From the line of David, virgin birth, name – Immanuel

2. Read Isaiah 11:1-9.

   a. Who is Isaiah describing in this passage?

   Jesus

   b. How do you know?

   Because He is described as from the family of David, some day be king, the Spirit of the Lord will be with him, greatest joy is obeying the Lord

3. Read Isaiah 42:1-9?

   a. Who is this passage about?

   Jesus

   b. How do you know?

   Because He is described as Chosen one, bringer of justice, has God's Spirit, sent by God

4. Read Isaiah 53:2-12.

   a. Who is Isaiah describing in this passage?

   Jesus

   b. How do you know?

   Because He is described as suffered for others' sins, condemned to death, asked God to forgive us

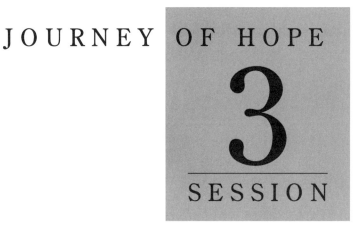

JOURNEY OF HOPE

3

SESSION

Isaiah's Message

OBJECTIVE

To discover the content of Isaiah's message to the Hebrew people and to apply this message to our daily lives.

READER

Chapter 3: Pain of a Prophet

LESSON PLAN

PRAYER

Opening prayer

REVIEW

Discuss students' responses to their Homework assignments from Session 2. Explain that these passages are known as Isaiah's messianic prophecies – they were prophecies about Jesus. Isaiah's messianic prophecies are an important example of Isaiah's one-item agenda – the holiness of God that we should have hope and faith in.

OBJECTIVE

State as described at left.

ACTIVITY

Distribute and explain the Activity worksheet for this session. Allow about 15-20 minutes to complete, and then discuss the students' findings.

CONNECTION

Next have students take the following notes.

Isaiah spoke and prophesied God's words to a rebellious and stubborn people. Isaiah's major messages about God's holiness were:

- That there is a future to work toward and hope for. To prepare us for that future God judges His people, which shows us how we need to "repent" and change our ways. (You may need to explain repent as "turning around and going the other way; turning away from sin and doing right.")

- That there is HOPE because God also comes to restore Israel and make her a holy people ready to serve God.

- That our greatest resource in times of trouble is FAITH and faithfulness – absolute trust in and dependence on God.

REFLECTION

Explain to students that they now have a chance to reflect on and apply Isaiah's messages to their own lives. Distribute the Reflection Questions worksheet.

ACTION

Complete any unfinished questions on the Reflection Questions worksheet for homework or have students read Chapter 3 in the *Journey of Hope Reader*.

SESSION 3: ISAIAH'S MESSAGE
ACTIVITY WORKSHEET

Name_____

Directions: Read the following Scripture passages and answer the questions below to help you discover more about Isaiah's messages to the Hebrew people.

1. Read Isaiah 6:9-10. In your own words summarize Isaiah's first message to the people. What does this message tell you about the people?

2. Read Isaiah 10:1-3 and summarize this message in your own words.

3. Read Isaiah 12:1-6 and summarize this message in your own words.

4. Read Isaiah 30:8-21 and summarize this message in your own words.

5. Read Isaiah 56:1-8 and summarize this message in your own words.

6. Read Isaiah 65:1-2 and summarize this message in your own words.

SESSION 3: ISAIAH'S MESSAGE
ACTIVITY WORKSHEET

TEACHER'S COPY

Directions: Read the following Scripture passages and answer the questions below to help you discover more about Isaiah's messages to the Hebrew people.

1. Read Isaiah 6:9-10. In your own words summarize Isaiah's first message to the people. What does this message tell you about the people?

Isaiah is telling the people that they really are not listening to or seeing how God is at work in their lives. The people were stubborn and self-centered.

2. Read Isaiah 10:1-3 and summarize this message in your own words.

The time is coming when the sinful people who have mistreated others will suffer negative consequences and have no help.

3. Read Isaiah 12:1-6 and summarize this message in your own words.

Isaiah is encouraging people to praise God for all the good He has done for them.

4. Read Isaiah 30:8-21 and summarize this message in your own words.

A warning to those who have turned against God and a reminder that if they but trust in God and return to God's way, that God will have mercy on them

5. Read Isaiah 56:1-8 and summarize this message in your own words.

A reminder that all people will be welcomed into God's people if they are honest, fair, obey God's commandments, and worship God

6. Read Isaiah 65:1-2 and summarize this message in your own words.

God is always reaching out to us, even when we aren't looking for Him.

SESSION 3 — ISAIAH'S MESSAGE
ACTIVITY WORKSHEET

Name_____

Reflection Questions

Directions: Reread all your notes on Isaiah. Then completely and seriously answer these questions.

Message 1

Isaiah's message – *There is a future, something to hope for, and God's judgment and call to repentance and change help us prepare for that future.*

1. If God were to judge you today, what would He say? Why?

2. What negative behaviors and influences do you need to "walk away from" (repent)? Explain.

3. What positive behaviors and influences do you need to "walk toward?" Explain.

Message 2

Isaiah's message – *There is hope! God comes to restore us and make us holy and fit to serve God.*

1. What does the word "restore" mean? (Use a dictionary, if necessary.)

2. What do you need God to restore in you? Why?

3. Which spiritual qualities do you need from God to help you become more holy?

SESSION 3 ACTIVITY WORKSHEET – PAGE 2

Message 3

Isaiah's message – *We have hope because God is with us.*

1. What does Isaiah mean by saying "God is with us"? How is God with us?

2. How is God with you? Explain.

3. What do you do need to do to help you pay closer attention to how God is with you in your daily life?

Message 4

Isaiah's message – *Faith in God is our greatest resource in times of trouble.*

1. Describe a time when your faith in God helped you through a rough time.

2. What could you do to grow more in your faith?

SESSION 3 ISAIAH'S MESSAGE
ACTIVITY WORKSHEET

TEACHER'S COPY

Reflection Questions

Directions: Reread all your notes on Isaiah. Then completely and seriously answer these questions.

Message 1

Isaiah's message – *There is a future, something to hope for, and God's judgment and call to repentance and change help us prepare for that future.*

1. If God were to judge you today, what would He say? Why?

Open-ended

2. What negative behaviors and influences do you need to "walk away from" (repent)? Explain.

Open-ended

3. What positive behaviors and influences do you need to "walk toward?" Explain.

Open-ended

Message 2

Isaiah's message – *There is hope! God comes to restore us and make us holy and fit to serve God.*

1. What does the word "restore" mean? (Use a dictionary, if necessary.)

Renew, rebuild, give new life to

2. What do you need God to restore in you? Why?

Open-ended

3. Which spiritual qualities do you need from God to help you become more holy?

Open-ended

SESSION 3 ACTIVITY WORKSHEET – PAGE 2   **TEACHER'S COPY**

Message 3

Isaiah's message – *We have hope because God is with us.*

1. What does Isaiah mean by saying "God is with us"? How is God with us?

God is with us in spirit, willing to give us the strength, love, forgiveness, and hope we need.

2. How is God with you? Explain.

Open-ended

3. What do you do need to do to help you pay closer attention to how God is with you in your daily life?

Open-ended

Message 4

Isaiah's message – *Faith in God is our greatest resource in times of trouble.*

1. Describe a time when your faith in God helped you through a rough time.

Open-ended

2. What could you do to grow more in your faith?

Open-ended

JOURNEY OF HOPE

SESSION 4

God's Promise of Hope and Healing

OBJECTIVE

To read and reflect on God's promise of hope and healing as found in the prophetic messages of Isaiah.

READER

Chapter 4: God's Promise of Hope and Healing

LESSON PLAN

PRAYER

Opening prayer

REVIEW

Discuss students' responses to the Reflection Questions worksheet from Session 3.

OBJECTIVE

State as described at left.

ACTIVITY

1. Divide the class into small groups of two or three. Assign each group one of the following passages:

    Isaiah 35 – The Road of Holiness

    Isaiah 58:6-12 – How God Wants Us to Treat Others

    Isaiah 61 – Good News of Deliverance

2. Explain that each group is to read their assigned passage and come up with a creative way to summarize and express God's promise of hope and healing in their passage. Some suggestions include:

- Crafting a poster (consisting of drawings, words, cut-out pictures, etc.) that depicts the theme of their passage.
- Compose and perform a song, poem, or rap that summarizes the message of their passage.
- Choose five to seven favorite verses from their passage and create a mini-poster of each verse. (Mini-poster would be a decorative, word-for-word quotation of that verse.)

3. Allow sufficient time for students to creatively depict their passage.

CONNECTION

Have each group present their passage project. While each group is presenting, instruct the rest of the class to take notes on each presentation. The notes should include:

- Presenters' names
- Scripture passage presented
- Description of two or three main themes presented

REFLECTION

Instruct students to review their notes and then choose their favorite passage of the three presented. Students are then to answer the following Reflection Questions based on that favorite passage.

1. Which of the three passages from Isaiah presented was your favorite? Explain why.

2. Re-read that passage and copy one or two verses from the passage that you like. Explain why you like each verse.

JOURNEY OF HOPE

SESSION 5

God Calls Jeremiah

OBJECTIVE

Students will read and discuss how Jeremiah discovered God's purpose for his life.

READER

Chapter 5: The Voice of God

LESSON PLAN

PRAYER

Opening prayer

REVIEW

Ask students to share their answers from their Reflection Questions from Session 4 regarding favorite passages from Isaiah. Next, review what they've learned about Isaiah by asking the following:

1. What was Isaiah's one-item agenda?
   God's holiness

2. Give examples of how Isaiah pointed to God's promise of hope and healing.

OBJECTIVE

Explain: *"Today we're going to begin to read about and discuss another prophet, Jeremiah. We'll begin by learning more about who he was, the times he lived in, and how he was called by God to be a prophet."*

ACTIVITY

1. Ask for a volunteer to read aloud the introduction to the book of Jeremiah as found in their Bibles.

2. Ask for another volunteer to read aloud Jeremiah 1:1-10. Use the following questions to discuss this passage.

   a. Approximately when did Jeremiah live?
   7th Century B.C.

   b. What was Jeremiah's father's name and what was his occupation?
   Hilkiah – priest

   c. What did the Lord say to Jeremiah in verses 4-5?
   I am your Creator and I chose you before you were born to be a prophet.

   d. What was Jeremiah's response?
   I don't how to speak; I am too young.

   e. What did the Lord do and say to Jeremiah in verse 9?
   Touched Jeremiah's mouth and gave him the words to speak

CONNECTION

Summarize by having students take the following notes about Jeremiah.

- Jeremiah was a prophet from 626 -586 B.C. – about 600 years before Jesus was born. He lived during a restless and uncertain time. The holy city of Jerusalem was eventually captured by the Babylonians in 587 B.C.

- Jeremiah was a young teen at the time of his call. He was afraid he would not know what to say and that he would not be listened to.

- Jeremiah found strength to overcome his fear in the power of God's word and discovered his true purpose was to be a "a prophet for the nations."

REFLECTION

Distribute and explain the Reflection Questions worksheet. Give time to complete.

ACTION

Distribute and explain the Homework worksheet.

SESSION 5 — GOD CALLS JEREMIAH
ACTIVITY WORKSHEET

Name_____

Reflection Questions

Directions: Read Jeremiah 1:4-10 and then answer the following questions.

1. When did God choose Jeremiah to be a prophet?

2. When and how did Jeremiah become aware of God's purpose for his life?

3. How do you think Jeremiah was feeling in verse 6? Why?

4. Copy verse 8 here:

© 2001 by Father Flanagan's Boys' Home.

JOURNEY OF HOPE

SESSION 5 ACTIVITY WORKSHEET – PAGE 2

5. How do you think Jeremiah felt when he heard what God said in verse 8? Why?

6. God has a purpose in mind for each of us. Do you know God's purpose for your life? Explain why or why not.

7. How are you like/unlike Jeremiah? Explain.

SESSION 5 — GOD CALLS JEREMIAH
ACTIVITY WORKSHEET

TEACHER'S COPY

Reflection Questions

Directions: Read Jeremiah 1:4-10 and then answer the following questions.

1. When did God choose Jeremiah to be a prophet?
Before Jeremiah was born

2. When and how did Jeremiah become aware of God's purpose for his life?
When Jeremiah was a young teen, the Lord God came to him in a vision and told Jeremiah of his purpose.

3. How do you think Jeremiah was feeling in verse 6? Why?
Open-ended

4. Copy verse 8 here:
I promise to be with you and keep you safe, so do not be afraid.

SESSION 5 ACTIVITY WORKSHEET – PAGE 2   **TEACHER'S COPY**

5. How do you think Jeremiah felt when he heard what God said in verse 8? Why?

Open-ended

6. God has a purpose in mind for each of us. Do you know God's purpose for your life? Explain why or why not.

Open-ended

7. How are you like/unlike Jeremiah? Explain.

Open-ended

SESSION 5 — GOD CALLS JEREMIAH
HOMEWORK

Name_____

Directions: Read the following passages from Jeremiah and answer the questions about each one.

1. Read Jeremiah 1:11-19.

   a. What did Jeremiah see in verse 11?

   b. What did the Lord say it meant? (verse 12)

   c. What did Jeremiah see in verse 13?

   d. What did the Lord say it meant? (verse 14)

   e. How had the people sinned? (verse 16)

SESSION 5 HOMEWORK – PAGE 2

    f.   What does the Lord promise Jeremiah in verses 18-19?

2. Read Jeremiah 2:20-25.

    a.   What does the Lord compare the people Israel to in verse 21?

    b.   What does the Lord mean by this comparison?

    c.   What does the Lord compare the people Israel to in verse 24?

    d.   What does the Lord mean by this comparison?

TEACHER'S COPY

Directions: Read the following passages from Jeremiah and answer the questions about each one.

1. Read Jeremiah 1:11-19.

   a. What did Jeremiah see in verse 11?

   Branch of almonds that ripened early

   b. What did the Lord say it meant? (verse 12)

   God rises early to keep a promise.

   c. What did Jeremiah see in verse 13?

   Pot of boiling water in the north about to spill out

   d. What did the Lord say it meant? (verse 14)

   God will bring destruction across the land.

   e. How had the people sinned? (verse 16)

   Turning away from God and worshiping false gods

SESSION 5 HOMEWORK – PAGE 2   **TEACHER'S COPY**

    f.   What does the Lord promise Jeremiah in verses 18-19?

        To give him the strength to speak God's message

2. Read Jeremiah 2:20-25.

    a.   What does the Lord compare the people Israel to in verse 21?

        A productive grapevine gone bad

    b.   What does the Lord mean by this comparison?

        That the people had turned away from God and were doing "bad" things by sinning

    c.   What does the Lord compare the people Israel to in verse 24?

        To a young female donkey in heat, willing to mate with anyone

    d.   What does the Lord mean by this comparison?

        That the people are fickle and unfaithful to God

JOURNEY OF HOPE

SESSION 6

Jeremiah's Messages

OBJECTIVE

To discover the content of God's messages spoken through Jeremiah to the people Israel and to apply these messages to our own lives.

READER

Chapter 6: Jeremiah's Messages

LESSON PLAN

PRAYER

Opening prayer

REVIEW

Discuss the Homework worksheet from the previous session.

OBJECTIVE

State as described at left.

ACTIVITY

1. On a table in the front of the room, display the following symbols used in the book of Jeremiah. (a pot, a branch, linen shorts, a piece of pottery, a basket of figs, a stuffed sheep/lamb)

2. Point to these symbols and explain: *"Each one is a symbol used in Jeremiah's messages to the people of Israel. A symbol is something that represents, or points to, a deeper meaning. You're now going to read*

more of the book of Jeremiah to see how God uses these symbols to reach and teach the people Israel."

3. Divide the class into five small groups. Assign each group one of the following passages:

    Jeremiah 3:6-25   Unfaithful Wife (Return to the Lord)

    Jeremiah 13:1-11   Linen Shorts (Destruction of Pride)

    Jeremiah 18:1-12   Pottery Shop (Punishment to Get Change)

    Jeremiah 24:1-10   Baskets of Figs (Return of the Exiles)

    Jeremiah 50:17-20   Sheep (Restoration of Exiles)

4. Next, distribute and explain the Activity worksheet. Allow at least 10-12 minutes to complete the worksheet.

CONNECTIONS

Have each small group present its findings to the class. Students should take the following notes on each presentation:

- Title, chapter, and verse of passage
- Symbol used
- What it symbolizes
- Main themes of the passage

REFLECTION

Distribute and explain Reflection Questions worksheet. Give class time to complete and/or finish for homework.

SESSION 6 — JEREMIAH'S MESSAGES
ACTIVITY WORKSHEET

Name_____

Group Activity

Have one person read aloud your assigned passage while the others follow along in their own Bibles.

Then, discuss and write answers to the questions below:

1. Write the title, chapter, and verses of your assigned passage here:

2. What symbol was used in this passage?

3. What was the symbol used to describe? Explain fully.

4. What was the main theme of this passage?

SESSION 6 ACTIVITY WORKSHEET – PAGE 2

5. What does this passage tell you about the people of Israel? Explain.

6. What can you learn about the Lord God from this passage? Explain.

Have one person of your group present your findings to the class.

SESSION 6 JEREMIAH'S MESSAGES
ACTIVITY WORKSHEET

TEACHER'S COPY

Group Activity

Have one person read aloud your assigned passage while the others follow along in their own Bibles.

Then, discuss and write answers to the questions below:

1. Write the title, chapter, and verses of your assigned passage here:

2. What symbol was used in this passage?
   a. *Jeremiah 3:6-25 Unfaithful Wife*
   b. *Jeremiah 13:1-11 Linen Shorts*
   c. *Jeremiah 18:1-12 Pottery Shop*
   d. *Jeremiah 24:1-10 Baskets of Figs*
   e. *Jeremiah 50:17-20 Sheep*

3. What was the symbol used to describe? Explain fully.
   a. *Unfaithful Wife – How Israel is unfaithful to God*
   b. *Linen Shorts – How close God wants to be to His people*
   c. *Pottery – Israel is like pottery molded by God, the master potter.*
   d. *Baskets of Figs – People of Israel who are rotten and people who will be saved*
   e. *Sheep – People of Israel who will be forgiven and restored*

4. What was the main theme of this passage?
   a. *Israel has been unfaithful to God. God wants to love and forgive Israel, if only Israel would change.*
   b. *God wants to be close to the people – as close as linen shorts, but the people of Israel refuse.*
   c. *God is like a Master Potter and the people of Israel are like the clay he shapes. God wants to shape and mold the people to be His own, but the people refuse to change.*

SESSION 6 ACTIVITY WORKSHEET – PAGE 2   **TEACHER'S COPY**

    d. *The people of Israel are like two baskets of figs – one rotten and one worth saving. God will save the worthwhile people and restore them.*

    e. *The people of Israel are like sheep scattered and lost. The Lord God promises to bring the people back and to nourish and restore them.*

5. What does this passage tell you about the people of Israel? Explain.

Each passage describes the people of Israel as sinful, stubborn, unwilling to repent.

6. What can you learn about the Lord God from this passage? Explain.

Each passage teaches us that the Lord God wants to love, forgive, and restore the people of Israel even though they have been unfaithful and sinful.

Have one person of your group present your findings to the class.

SESSION 6 JEREMIAH'S MESSAGES
ACTIVITY WORKSHEET

Name_____

Reflection Questions

1. Choose one of your favorite symbols from Jeremiah's messages and explain what the symbol can teach us about:

   a. The people Israel:

   b. God:

2. Jeremiah lived in a restless and uncertain time. Name some ways the world we live in today is like Jeremiah's times.

SESSION 6 ACTIVITY WORKSHEET – PAGE 2

3. Which of Jeremiah's messages would most apply to people today? Why?

4. Which of Jeremiah's messages apply most to you? Why?

JOURNEY OF HOPE

SESSION 7

Jeremiah: The New Covenant

LESSON PLAN

OBJECTIVE
In this session, students will discover how Isaiah discovered God's purpose for his life.

READER
Chapter 7: Broken Covenants

PRAYER

Opening prayer

REVIEW

Use Reflection Questions worksheet from Session 6 as a discussion tool to review what they've learned about Jeremiah.

OBJECTIVE

Explain: *"In today's session we'll explore in depth Jeremiah's one-item agenda – the new Covenant between God and the people Israel. A covenant is an agreement between two unequal parties. One party dictates the terms and conditions to which the other must agree to live by."*

ACTIVITY

Present a mini-lecture based on Jeremiah 31:31-34. Students should take notes on this mini-lecture.

> Jeremiah's one-item agenda was the New Covenant between God and the people Israel.

This New Covenant:

- Begins with the authority of God. God initiates this promise. Israel is invited to respond to God's initiatives. (verse 31)

- Is a restatement of the Mosaic covenant. The Laws of the Mosaic covenant, the Ten Commandments, were written on stone tablets. This New Covenant will be written on our hearts by God. (verses 32-33)

- Will challenge each person to respond to God personally, in daily life, by living out the commandments. (verse 34)

- States that "I will be your God, you will be my people" (verse 33), and it will renew the community of faith one by one.

- Is based on God's forgiveness of sins, allowing us a fresh start, a new beginning. (verse 34) God's forgiveness is given after the discipline for our wrongdoing and is the kind of discipline meant to "tear down" selfish pride and "build up" a people fit to serve God.

- Announces the beginning of a new age – an age that will find fulfillment in the life, death, and resurrection of Jesus Christ.

This New Covenant was necessary because the people Israel had not understood it previously. God, through grace, gives us the same message in a new way.

CONNECTION/REFLECTION

Explain to students that this activity will help them to apply the elements of the New Covenant to their own relationship with God. Distribute and explain the Activity worksheet for this session. Give them time to complete it.

ACTION

Complete any unfinished portions of the Activity worksheet or read Chapter 7 in the *Journey of Hope Reader*.

JEREMIAH: THE NEW COVENANT
ACTIVITY WORKSHEET

Name_____

Directions: Re-read your notes from this session and read Jeremiah 31:31-34. Then complete the following activities and questions.

PART 1: Questions

1. What is this new covenant the Lord says He will make? (verses 31-33)

2. According to your notes:

  a. What is a "covenant"?

  b. List below five synonyms for "covenant" as found in a thesaurus.

  1. _____   4. _____
  2. _____   5. _____
  3. _____

3. How is this New Covenant different from the old covenant? (verses 32-33)

4. What does God promise to write on our hearts? (verse 33)

5. What does God promise to give us? (verse 34)

6. Describe the way God disciplines. (from notes)

© 2001 by Father Flanagan's Boys' Home.

JOURNEY OF HOPE

SESSION 7 ACTIVITY WORKSHEET – PAGE 2

PART 2: Activity

Directions: Read the passage from Jeremiah below and complete the following activities.

"Here is the new agreement that I, the Lord, will make with the people of Israel: I will write my laws on their hearts and minds. I will be their God and they will be my people."
– Jeremiah 31:33

1. What is the law of God that is to be written on our hearts? Read the following Scripture passages to find out.

   a. Read Matthew 22:37-40. What are the two great commandments of the Law?

   b. Read Luke 10:25-37. Who must we love in order to receive eternal life?

   c. Who is your neighbor?

2. Name three examples of ways you can show that you love God above all else.
   a.

   b.

   c.

3. Name three ways you can love your neighbor as you love yourself.
   a.

   b.

   c.

© 2001 by Father Flanagan's Boys' Home.

JOURNEY OF HOPE

SESSION 7 ACTIVITY WORKSHEET – PAGE 3

4. God says that He will put His law within each of us and will write it on our hearts and minds. Sometimes our hearts get dirtied with sin, hurt, anger, and resentments. Sometimes we need to say to God, *"Create in me a clean heart, O God, and renew a right Spirit within me."* (Psalm 51)

   a. Draw a heart below. Inside the heart describe the things that are "dirtying" your heart right now. Which of these things would you like God to remove (wipe clean) from your heart? Why?

   b. Now draw a second heart. Inside this heart write the positive qualities you would like God to place in your newly cleansed heart.
   (Read Colossians 3:12-17 for ideas.)

SESSION 7 — JEREMIAH: THE NEW COVENANT
ACTIVITY WORKSHEET

TEACHER'S COPY

Directions: Re-read your notes from this session and read Jeremiah 31:31-34. Then complete the following activities and questions.

PART 1: Questions

1. What is this new covenant the Lord says He will make? (verses 31-33)

"I will write my laws on their hearts and minds. I will be their God, and they will be my people."

2. According to your notes:

a. What is a "covenant"?

A covenant is an agreement between two unequal parties. One party dictates the terms and conditions to which the other must agree to live by.

b. List below five synonyms for "covenant" as found in a thesaurus.

1. *promise*
2. *agreement*
3. *contract*
4. *bond*
5. *pact*

3. How is this New Covenant different from the old covenant? (verses 32-33)

It will be written in our minds and in our hearts.

4. What does God promise to write on our hearts? (verse 33)

His laws

5. What does God promise to give us? (verse 34)

Forgiveness of sins and the ability to obey God

6. Describe the way God disciplines. (from notes)

God's forgiveness is given after discipline for wrongdoings. It is the kind of discipline meant to "tear down" selfish pride and "build up" a people fit to serve God.

SESSION 7 ACTIVITY WORKSHEET – PAGE 2   **TEACHER'S COPY**

PART 2: Activity

Directions: Read the passage from Jeremiah below and complete the following activities.

"Here is the new agreement that I, the Lord, will make with the people of Israel: I will write my laws on their hearts and minds. I will be their God and they will be my people."

– Jeremiah 31:33

1. What is the law of God that is to be written on our hearts? Read the following Scripture passages to find out.

   a. Read Matthew 22:37-40. What are the two great commandments of the Law?

   1. *Love God with all your heart, soul, and mind.*
   2. *Love others as much as you love yourself.*

   b. Read Luke 10:25-37. Who must we love in order to receive eternal life?

   Our neighbors

   c. Who is your neighbor?

   Everyone, especially those we don't consider worthy of being our neighbor

2. Name three examples of ways you can show that you love God above all else.

   a. *Open-ended*

   b. *Open-ended*

   c. *Open-ended*

3. Name three ways you can love your neighbor as you love yourself.

   a. *Open-ended*

   b. *Open-ended*

   c. *Open-ended*

SESSION 7 ACTIVITY WORKSHEET – PAGE 3   **TEACHER'S COPY**

4. God says that He will put His law within each of us and will write it on our hearts and minds. Sometimes our hearts get dirtied with sin, hurt, anger, and resentments. Sometimes we need to say to God, *"Create in me a clean heart, O God, and renew a right Spirit within me."* (Psalm 51)

   a. Draw a heart below. Inside the heart describe the things that are "dirtying" your heart right now. Which of these things would you like God to remove (wipe clean) from your heart? Why?

   b. Now draw a second heart. Inside this heart write the positive qualities you would like God to place in your newly cleansed heart.
   (Read Colossians 3:12-17 for ideas.)

JOURNEY OF HOPE

8

SESSION

Lamentations: Handling Hardships

OBJECTIVE

Students will read, reflect on, and discuss segments of the book of Lamentations in order to discover how to best handle hardships and suffering in life.

READER

Chapter 8: Handling Hardships

LESSON PLAN

PRAYER

Opening prayer

REVIEW

Review student responses to the worksheet from the previous session.

OBJECTIVE

Explain: *"Today we will read, reflect on, and discuss segments of the book of Lamentations in order to gain a new perspective on how to handle life's hardships and suffering."*

CONNECTION

Explain: *"Before reading Lamentations, there are a few items that need further clarification. Let's take a few notes to help us better understand what we're about to read."*

- The book of Lamentations was written by the prophet Jeremiah to express the sorrow and suffering experienced by the people of Israel after the destruction of Jerusalem in 586 B.C.

- The word "Lamentations" means feeling or expressing deep sadness and sorrow.
- The first few chapters of Lamentations are full of self-pity. Occasionally the people of Israel were prone to feeling very sorry for themselves. Jeremiah, however, puts a different spin on their lamenting. He challenges them to change their focus from self-pity to remembering the Lord's steadfast love and mercy and reminding them to put their hope and trust in the Lord.

ACTIVITY

1. Ask for ten volunteers who will read aloud the following passages from Lamentations. Explain that these passages are divided into three separate groups and will be read as follows:

    - Group 1 – What Jerusalem was like after the destruction

        Lamentations 1:1-5

        Lamentations 1:6-8

    - Group 2 – What life was like for the people after the fall of Jerusalem

        Lamentations 2:10-12

        Lamentations 4:1-5

        Lamentations 5:2-6

        Lamentations 5:9-18

    - Group 3 – How the people should respond to their suffering

        Lamentations 3:17-24

        Lamentations 3:25-26

        Lamentations 3:27-31

        Lamentations 3:55-58

2. Instruct readers that when reading aloud they should:
   - Stand.
   - Face the class.
   - State chapter and verse to be read.
   - Read slowly.
   - Speak clearly.

3. Direct the other students that when listening they should:
   - Look at the reader.
   - Listen closely.
   - Have Bible open to passage being read.
   - After each passage, complete the corresponding segment of the worksheet.

4. Distribute Activity worksheets. Invite volunteers forward, one at a time, to read passages. Pause between readings so class may write answers on the worksheet.

5. After students have read all ten passages, discuss their responses.

REFLECTION

Distribute the Reflection worksheet for this session and allow time for students to begin. Students should finish the worksheet for homework.

SESSION 8 LAMENTATIONS: HANDLING HARDSHIPS
HOMEWORK

Name_____

Reflection Worksheet

Directions: Review your answers from the Activity worksheet from this session. Create a poem, prayer, song, cartoon, or poster that communicates Jeremiah's response to suffering as named in Lamentations 3:17-24, 25-31, or 55-58. Possible themes might be:

1. How to handle suffering appropriately

2. Next time I feel sorry for myself I should...

3. No matter how bad it gets I need to remember...

SESSION 8
LAMENTATIONS: HANDLING HARDSHIPS
ACTIVITY WORKSHEET

Name_____

Directions: After each passage is read aloud, read and answer the question next to the passage.

PART 1: What Jerusalem was like after the destruction

1. Lamentations 1:1-4 – What words or phrases are used to describe Jerusalem?

2. Lamentations 1:6-8 – What words or phrases are used to describe Jerusalem's leaders?

PART 2: What life was like for the people after the fall of Jerusalem

3. Lamentations 2:10-12 – Describe how the people are behaving now that Jerusalem has fallen.

4. Lamentations 4:1-5 – What is happening to the children?

5. Lamentations 5:2-6 – What has happened to their property?

6. Lamentations 5:9-17 – What crimes are being committed against them?

© 2001 by Father Flanagan's Boys' Home.

JOURNEY OF HOPE

SESSION 8 ACTIVITY WORKSHEET – PAGE 2

PART 3: How the people should respond to their suffering

7. Lamentations 3:17-24 – Who can always be trusted to show mercy?

8. Lamentations 3:25-27 – When is it best to learn patience and struggle hard?

9. Lamentations 3:28-31 – What should people do when they suffer?

10. Lamentations 3:55-58 – When we're "in the pits" what should we do?

SESSION 8 — LAMENTATIONS: HANDLING HARDSHIPS
ACTIVITY WORKSHEET

TEACHER'S COPY

Directions: After each passage is read aloud, read and answer the question next to the passage.

PART 1: What Jerusalem was like after the destruction

1. Lamentations 1:1-4 – What words or phrases are used to describe Jerusalem?

Like a widow, a slave, betrayed by friends, sinful

2. Lamentations 1:6-8 – What words or phrases are used to describe Jerusalem's leaders?

Like deer that can't find pasture, suffering, scattered, hunted, disgraced

PART 2: What life was like for the people after the fall of Jerusalem

3. Lamentations 2:10-12 – Describe how the people are behaving now that Jerusalem has fallen.

Leaders are silent and in mourning, crying, sad, depressed, starving.

4. Lamentations 4:1-5 – What is happening to the children?

Treated like they are worthless, starving, thirsty, and abandoned

5. Lamentations 5:2-6 – What has happened to their property?

Property has been taken by foreigners and strangers, can't afford water or wood to burn

6. Lamentations 5:9-17 – What crimes are being committed against them?

Attacked by desert tribes, women raped, rulers tortured, young men are slaves

SESSION 8 ACTIVITY WORKSHEET – PAGE 2   **TEACHER'S COPY**

PART 3: How the people should respond to their suffering

7. Lamentations 3:17-24 – Who can always be trusted to show mercy?
The Lord

8. Lamentations 3:25-27 – When is it best to learn patience and struggle hard?
When we are young

9. Lamentations 3:28-31 – What should people do when they suffer?
Learn from it and turn to the Lord

10. Lamentations 3:55-58 – When we're "in the pits" what should we do?
Pray to God, ask for God's help.

JOURNEY OF HOPE
SESSION 9

God Calls Ezekiel

OBJECTIVE

Students will read and discuss how Ezekiel received God's call to be a prophet.

READER

Chapter 9: Accepting Responsibility

LESSON PLAN

PRAYER

Opening prayer

REVIEW

Ask for volunteers to describe how Jeremiah and Isaiah received God's call to be a prophet.

OBJECTIVE

State as described at left.

ACTIVITY

1. Ask for a volunteer to read the introduction to the book of Ezekiel as found in their Bible. Clarify any questions that come from the introduction.

2. Next, ask for volunteers to read aloud Ezekiel 2 through 3:15.

3. Use the following questions to discuss the passage.

   a. What does God call Ezekiel?
   Mortal man

b. Why does God call him this?
To remind Ezekiel who he is and who God is, who is the Creator, and who is the Creature

c. Who did God send Ezekiel to speak to? Why?
To the people Israel, because they had rebelled and turned against God

d. What does Ezekiel eating God's scroll symbolize?
That Ezekiel must fill himself with the Word of God, it must become part of him

e. According to Ezekiel, how did the scroll taste?
Sweet as honey

f. What does this symbolize?
That the Word of God is good

CONNECTION

Summarize all the information about Ezekiel by having the students take the following notes:

- Like Jeremiah and Isaiah, Ezekiel was called by God to become a prophet. Ezekiel's purpose was to speak God's word to the people Israel.

- Ezekiel was one of many prominent Israelites who were taken from Jerusalem and forced to live in exile in Babylon. Ezekiel knew what it was like to be far from home and to be separated from friends and family.

- Like Isaiah and Jeremiah, God sent Ezekiel to preach to the rebellious and stubborn Israelites. Just like the prophets before him, God promised to give Ezekiel the words to say and the strength to say them.

- Ezekiel's one-item agenda was individual responsibility and individual faith. Ezekiel urged people to take responsibility and stop putting other things in God's place. He wanted people to realize that only God can give meaning to life.

REFLECTION

Distribute and explain the Reflection Questions worksheet. Give time to complete.

SESSION 9 — GOD CALLS EZEKIEL
ACTIVITY WORKSHEET

Name_____

Reflection Questions

Directions: Use your notes from today's session, as well as Ezekiel 2 through 3:15 to help you answer these questions.

1. What was God's purpose for Ezekiel?

2. Why does God address Ezekiel as "Son of man"? (See footnote n, p. 855)

3. What did God give Ezekiel to eat? Why? What did this symbolize?

4. Write 20 words or phrases that describe Ezekiel.

© 2001 by Father Flanagan's Boys' Home.

JOURNEY OF HOPE

SESSION 9 ACTIVITY WORKSHEET – PAGE 2

5. How are you like/unlike Ezekiel? Explain.

6. How are you like/unlike the people of Israel that Ezekiel was sent to speak to? Explain.

SESSION 9 GOD CALLS EZEKIEL
ACTIVITY WORKSHEET

TEACHER'S COPY

Reflection Questions

Directions: Use your notes from today's session, as well as Ezekiel 2 through 3:15 to help you answer these questions.

1. What was God's purpose for Ezekiel?

To become a prophet

2. Why does God address Ezekiel as "Son of man"? (See footnote n, p. 855)

To remind Ezekiel that God is the immortal Creator and that Ezekiel is a mortal man created by God and chosen to preach God's message

3. What did God give Ezekiel to eat? Why? What did this symbolize?

A scroll – symbolized God giving him the prophetic words to speak

4. Write 20 words or phrases that describe Ezekiel.

Examples:	*son of man*	*stubborn*	*created by God*
	determined	*prophet*	*sent by God*
	shocked	*Spirit-filled*	

105

SESSION 9 ACTIVITY WORKSHEET – PAGE 2   **TEACHER'S COPY**

5. How are you like/unlike Ezekiel? Explain.
Open-ended

6. How are you like/unlike the people of Israel that Ezekiel was sent to speak to? Explain.
Open-ended

JOURNEY OF HOPE

10

SESSION

Ezekiel's Warnings

OBJECTIVE

To enable students to read, discuss, and apply to their own lives the prophetic warnings of Ezekiel.

READER

Chapter 10: Consequences of Infidelity to God

LESSON PLAN

PRAYER

Opening prayer

REVIEW

Discuss the Reflection Questions worksheet from Session 9 to review what they've learned so far about Ezekiel.

OBJECTIVE

State as described at left.

ACTIVITY

Explain that this activity will help them to better understand the sinfulness of the people of Israel and the many warnings and signs God gave them through Ezekiel.

1. Divide the class into small groups.
2. Assign each group one of the following passages:

   Ezekiel 4:1-17

   Ezekiel 5:1-12

   Ezekiel 12:1-16

3. Instruct each group to read their passage, and then discuss and write answers to the questions on the accompanying Activity worksheet.

4. Have one person from each small group present its findings to the class.

CONNECTION

Have students take the following notes to summarize what they've learned so far.

- God gave the people Israel many signs and warnings through the prophet Ezekiel, but most refused to change their ways.

- The people Israel were guilty of idolatry – turning away from God and worshiping false gods. They were guilty of making other things more important than God.

- The consequence of their sinfulness and unwillingness to repent was separation from God.

REFLECTION

Instruct students to complete the Reflection Questions worksheet as a way of applying what they've learned so far to their own lives.

ACTION

Direct each student to write a paragraph or two describing a creative way Ezekiel could warn the people of today to stop sinning and return to God.

SESSION 10 EZEKIEL'S WARNINGS
ACTIVITY WORKSHEET

Name_____

Directions: Read your assigned passage from Ezekiel and then answer the following questions:

1. Describe what God asks Ezekiel to do in this passage.

2. What is God's purpose for asking Ezekiel to do this?

3. What sins have the people Israel committed?

4. What will be the consequence of their sin?

SESSION 10: EZEKIEL'S WARNINGS
ACTIVITY WORKSHEET

TEACHER'S COPY

Directions: Read your assigned passage from Ezekiel and then answer the following questions:

1. Describe what God asks Ezekiel to do in this passage.

Ezekiel 4:1-17 – Act out an attack on Jerusalem

Ezekiel 5:1-12 – Cut off his hair and beard and burn them

Ezekiel 12:1-16 – Act out Israel's exile and captivity

2. What is God's purpose for asking Ezekiel to do this?

Ezekiel 4:1-17 – A warning to the people of Israel demonstrating how they will suffer for their sins

Ezekiel 5:1-12 – To warn Jerusalem of coming destruction that will spread like a destroying fire

Ezekiel 12:1-16 – To show the people what will happen when they are taken away as prisoners

3. What sins have the people Israel committed?

Ezekiel 4:1-17 – Not specified in this passage

Ezekiel 5:1-12 – Rebelled against God; refused to obey His laws

Ezekiel 12:1-16 – Refused to see or listen to God's ways

4. What will be the consequence of their sin?

Ezekiel 4:1-17 – They will be starving, afraid, hopeless, and will die a slow death.

Ezekiel 5:1-12 – They will die of disease and starvation, be killed in war, or scattered and killed. God will turn His back on them.

Ezekiel 12:1-16 – People will be forced to live as exiles in foreign nations. Some will die of disease, starvation, or in war.

SESSION 10 EZEKIEL'S WARNINGS
ACTIVITY WORKSHEET

Name_____

Reflection Questions

1. Ezekiel's messages to the people of Israel warned them to change their ways, to repent, and return to God. If God were to send Ezekiel to the world today, what warnings would he give us? Why?

2. The people of Israel were guilty of idolatry – making other things more important than God. What are some things that you sometimes let become more important than God in your life? Why?

3. The consequence of sin is separation from God. Have you ever experienced feeling separated from God? Explain why or why not.

JOURNEY OF HOPE

SESSION 11

Ezekiel's Messages of Hope

LESSON PLAN

OBJECTIVE

Students will read, discuss, and apply to their own lives Ezekiel's prophetic messages of hope.

READER

Chapter 11: A Message of Hope to Those in Exile

PRAYER

Opening prayer

REVIEW

Ask for volunteers to read and explain their Reflection Questions from Session 10 (creative ways Ezekiel could warn people today to repent).

OBJECTIVE

State as described at left.

ACTIVITY

1. Present the following information as a mini-lecture. Have the students take notes.

   - Ezekiel's warnings to the people Israel for the most part went unheeded. Most people did not change their ways. They continued to rebel against God. And because of their cold-heartedness, they suffered spiritual separation from God.

113

- Ezekiel's prophesies of doom were realized when Jerusalem fell under siege in 586 B.C. Now the people of Israel suffered even more physical and spiritual separation from God.
- After the fall of Jerusalem, Ezekiel's messages changed. His message became one of assurance and hope for a people under siege.

2. In order to help students discover Ezekiel's messages of hope, have them complete the Activity worksheet for this session.

CONNECTION

Discuss their findings on the Activity worksheet.

REFLECTION

Complete the Reflection Questions worksheet for homework.

SESSION 11 — EZEKIEL'S MESSAGES OF HOPE

ACTIVITY WORKSHEET

Name_____

Directions: Read the following passages from Ezekiel. Then answer the questions about each passage.

1. Read Ezekiel 18:21-32.

  a. What does God say will happen to someone who is evil but stops sinning?

  b. What does God say will happen to a good person who stops doing good and starts doing evil?

  c. How does God say He will judge us? (verse 30)

2. Read Ezekiel 34:11-15.

  a. Who does God compare Himself to?

  b. Who does God compare people to?

  c. According to this passage, how does God say He will treat people?

SESSION 11 ACTIVITY WORKSHEET – PAGE 2

3. Read Ezekiel 36:26-28.

    a. In verse 26, God says He will give us a new H_____ and a desire to be F_____ .

    b. In verse 27, God says he will put in us His Spirit so that we will be eager to do what?

4. Read Ezekiel 37:1-14.

    a. What does God instruct Ezekiel to tell the dry bones?

    b. What does God cause to happen to the dry bones?

    c. Who does God say are like these dry bones? (verses 11-15) Explain why.

SESSION 11: EZEKIEL'S MESSAGES OF HOPE
ACTIVITY WORKSHEET

TEACHER'S COPY

Directions: Read the following passages from Ezekiel. Then answer the questions about each passage.

1. Read Ezekiel 18:21-32.

   a. What does God say will happen to someone who is evil but stops sinning?

   God will save them.

   b. What does God say will happen to a good person who stops doing good and starts doing evil?

   God will condemn them.

   c. How does God say He will judge us? (verse 30)

   On what we do – our behaviors

2. Read Ezekiel 34:11-15.

   a. Who does God compare Himself to?

   Shepherd

   b. Who does God compare people to?

   Sheep

   c. According to this passage, how does God say He will treat people?

   Take care of, keep safe, bring back the lost, heal the wounded, protect the weak

SESSION 11 ACTIVITY WORKSHEET – PAGE 2 **TEACHER'S COPY**

3. Read Ezekiel 36:26-28.

    a. In verse 26, God says He will give us a new H*eart*_____ and a desire to be F*aithful*_____ .

    b. In verse 27, God says he will put in us His Spirit so that we will be eager to do what?

    Obey God's laws and teachings

4. Read Ezekiel 37:1-14.

    a. What does God instruct Ezekiel to tell the dry bones?

    That the Lord God will put breath in you and you will live again

    b. What does God cause to happen to the dry bones?

    Covers them with muscle and skin; breathes life into them

    c. Who does God say are like these dry bones? (verses 11-15) Explain why.

    The people of Israel, because God promises to breath new life into them, to set them free from oppression, and bring them home

Name_____

Reflection Questions

Directions: Review your notes and your Activity worksheet for this session before answering these Reflection Questions.

1. In Ezekiel 18:21-32, we heard that God will judge each of us according to what we have done in our lives. If God were to judge your life so far, what would He find? Explain why.

2. In Ezekiel 34:11-15 God says He will care for us like a shepherd cares for his sheep. Read the encyclopedia or other resource book to discover exactly how a shepherd cares for his sheep. Write five specific examples below:

   a.   A shepherd cares for his sheep by...

   b.   A shepherd cares for his sheep by...

   c.   A shepherd cares for his sheep by...

   d.   A shepherd cares for his sheep by...

   e.   A shepherd cares for his sheep by...

SESSION 11 HOMEWORK – PAGE 2

3. From what you discovered about what shepherds do for their sheep, what does this tell you about what God will do for us?

4. In Ezekiel 36:26-28, God says He will replace our stubborn hearts with a new heart, full of the desire to be faithful, empowered by the Holy Spirit.

   a. In what ways has your heart become stubborn or hardened toward God? Why?

   b. Describe the kind of heart and mind you need God to give you. Why?

   c. How could having God's Spirit within you help you? Explain.

5. How are you like/unlike the dry bones in Ezekiel 37? Explain.

SESSION 11 — EZEKIEL'S MESSAGES OF HOPE
HOMEWORK

TEACHER'S COPY

Reflection Questions

Directions: Review your notes and your Activity worksheet for this session before answering these Reflection Questions.

1. In Ezekiel 18:21-32, we heard that God will judge each of us according to what we have done in our lives. If God were to judge your life so far, what would He find? Explain why.

Open-ended

2. In Ezekiel 34:11-15 God says He will care for us like a shepherd cares for his sheep. Read the encyclopedia or other resource book to discover exactly how a shepherd cares for his sheep. Write five specific examples below:

a. A shepherd cares for his sheep by...
protecting them from attacking animals.

b. A shepherd cares for his sheep by...
bringing back any lost sheep.

c. A shepherd cares for his sheep by...
guarding them from being stolen.

d. A shepherd cares for his sheep by...
examining them for wounds or disease and treating them.

e. A shepherd cares for his sheep by...
counting and keeping track of each one.

SESSION 11 HOMEWORK – PAGE 2 **TEACHER'S COPY**

3. From what you discovered about what shepherds do for their sheep, what does this tell you about what God will do for us?

God, like a Shepherd, will protect us, bring the lost back to Him, care for us, etc.

4. In Ezekiel 36:26-28, God says He will replace our stubborn hearts with a new heart, full of the desire to be faithful, empowered by the Holy Spirit.

　a. In what ways has your heart become stubborn or hardened toward God? Why?
　Open-ended

　b. Describe the kind of heart and mind you need God to give you. Why?
　Open-ended

　c. How could having God's Spirit within you help you? Explain.
　Open-ended

5. How are you like/unlike the dry bones in Ezekiel 37? Explain.
Open-ended

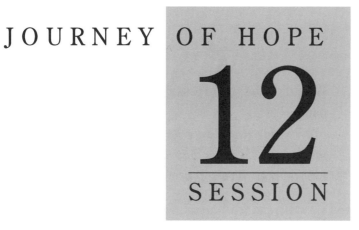

JOURNEY OF HOPE
SESSION 12

Hosea

OBJECTIVE
Students will become familiar with, discuss, and analyze the book of Hosea.

READER
Chapter 12: Called Back to Fidelity

LESSON PLAN

PRAYER

Opening prayer

REVIEW

Discuss student responses to the Reflection Questions worksheet from the previous session.

OBJECTIVE

State as described at left.

ACTIVITY

1. Distribute the handout, "List of Characters," for this session. Use this handout to explain who's who in the book of Hosea.

2. Next ask for volunteers to read aloud the introduction to Hosea and chapters 1 and 2. Use the following questions to discuss the scripture.

   a. What was the problem in Hosea's marriage?
   Gomer's infidelity

123

b. Why did God give Hosea's children such odd names?
Each name was a sign for the people to repent. This may seem odd to us, but was common practice in the Hebrew culture that the meaning of your name gave you a new identity.

c. Explain the comparison between Gomer and the people Israel.
Just like Gomer was unfaithful to her husband, Hosea, the people Israel were unfaithful to God.

d. How does God respond to Israel's infidelity?
In chapter 2:19-23, God promises to be true, faithful, and show steadfast love and mercy to the people Israel, even though they have been unfaithful.

CONNECTION

Have students take the following notes on the prophet Hosea:

- Hosea amplifies a theme of Isaiah, Ezekiel, and Jeremiah – Israel has sinned and needs to repent and return to the Lord. Hosea prophesies a message of pending doom and destruction as a consequence for Israel's sin. Even his children's names are signs of the negative consequences to come because of the people's sinfulness.

- Hosea's most powerful message – his one-item agenda – is how much God loves his people and wants his people to repent of their sins and come back to Him.

- The book of Hosea is unique because it compares God's unconditional love for His unfaithful people to Hosea's love for his unfaithful wife. Hosea is the first prophet to use the image of the marriage covenant to describe God's love for us.

REFLECTION

Distribute the Reflection Questions worksheet. Have students complete individually.

SESSION 12 — HOSEA HANDOUT

Hosea: List of Characters

Hosea A prophet, lived about 721 B.C. Married, with three children.

Gomer Wife of Hosea, mother of three children, guilty of unfaithfulness in her marriage.

Jezreel Eldest male child of Hosea and Gomer. God gave him this name to be a sign to the people that those who sin will reap negative consequences.

"Unloved" Second child of Hosea and Gomer, a daughter. God gave her this name to remind the people Israel that God's patience for their sinful ways was exhausted.

"Not My People" Third child of Hosea and Gomer, a son. God gave him this name to remind the people Israel that they had broken their covenant relationship with God.

© 2001 by Father Flanagan's Boys' Home.

JOURNEY OF HOPE

SESSION 12 — HOSEA
ACTIVITY WORKSHEET

Name_____

Reflection Questions

1. Describe how the people Israel and Gomer were alike.

2. Describe how you are like/unlike Gomer and Israel in your relationship with God.

3. How, in your life, has God shown you His steadfast love and mercy?

4. If Hosea, Gomer, and their three children lived today, what names might God give these children to serve as warnings to today's society about our evil and sinful ways? Explain your answer.

SESSION 12 HOSEA
ACTIVITY WORKSHEET

TEACHER'S COPY

Reflection Questions

1. Describe how the people Israel and Gomer were alike.

   Both were unfaithful in their relationships. Gomer was unfaithful in her marriage to Hosea by having sexual relations outside of marriage. Israel was unfaithful to God by worshiping false gods and by not following God's ways.

2. Describe how you are like/unlike Gomer and Israel in your relationship with God.

   Open-ended

3. How, in your life, has God shown you His steadfast love and mercy?

   Open-ended

4. If Hosea, Gomer, and their three children lived today, what names might God give these children to serve as warnings to today's society about our evil and sinful ways? Explain your answer.

   Open-ended

JOURNEY OF HOPE
SESSION 13

Hosea: God's Love Is 'Hessed'

LESSON PLAN

OBJECTIVE

In this session, students will discover and apply to their own lives the prophetic messages of Hosea.

READER

Chapter 13: God's Compassion

PRAYER

Opening prayer

REVIEW

Discuss students' responses to the Reflection Questions from Session 12.

OBJECTIVE

Explain: *"In today's session, we're going to discover more of what Hosea can teach us about God's love for us."*

ACTIVITY

Explain: *"This Scripture search will help you discover four important lessons Hosea can teach us about God."*

Distribute the Activity worksheet for this session to students and allow time to complete.

CONNECTION

Discuss their answers to the Activity worksheet. Then have students take the following notes.

Four lessons about God from Hosea:

- God's love is "Hessed" – Hessed is Hebrew for steadfast love. We should return this kind of love to God.

- The people Israel did not "know" God with their hearts and this was the cause of all their problems. The people Israel needed to learn how to recognize and understand who God is, what God has done for us, and what God requires of us. So do we.

- In recognizing and acknowledging who God is, we are called to respond to God. In this recognition and response to God, we begin to discover God's purpose for us.

- God's love surpasses human love. It is better and more complete than we can even imagine. God's love is so awesome that it is beyond our understanding. God's love has two important components – judgment and restoration. His judgment calls us to accountability for our sins and failings. Restoration includes God's forgiveness of our sins and the gift of the Holy Spirit to enable us to be better, more holy, live more righteously than before.

REFLECTION

Instruct each student to create an acrostic describing "God's love" using words and phrases learned today. Examples:

Given freely	**H**eavenly
bey**O**nd understanding	**E**ternal
ju**D**ges and	**S**urpasses
re**S**tores	con**S**tant
unconditiona**L**	r**E**news
c**O**nstant	un**D**ying
gi**V**en to All	
Eternal	

SESSION 13
HOSEA: GOD'S LOVE IS 'HESSED'
ACTIVITY WORKSHEET

Name_____

Directions: Read the following passages from Hosea and answer the questions below to discover four important things about God!

1. Read Hosea 6:1-6.

    a. What do the people decide to do in verses 1-3?

    b. What is the Lord's frustration with the people? (verse 4)

    c. What does God want from people? (verse 6)

2. Read Hosea 13:4.
    Who does God say that He is?

© 2001 by Father Flanagan's Boys' Home.

JOURNEY OF HOPE

SESSION 13 ACTIVITY WORKSHEET – PAGE 2

3. Read Hosea 2:19-23.

    a. What does God promise to give to Israel in verses 19-20?

    b. What are the people Israel to answer in response to God's promises? (verse 23)

4. Read Hosea 11:1-9.

    a. To what does the Lord compare His love for Israel? (verse 1)

    b. How did Israel respond to God's love? (verse 2)

    c. What does God promise in verses 8-9?

SESSION 13 — HOSEA: GOD'S LOVE IS 'HESSED'
ACTIVITY WORKSHEET

TEACHER'S COPY

Directions: Read the following passages from Hosea and answer the questions below to discover four important things about God!

1. Read Hosea 6:1-6.

    a. What do the people decide to do in verses 1-3?

    To return to the Lord and His ways and to come to know the Lord

    b. What is the Lord's frustration with the people? (verse 4)

    That they are fickle – their love for God comes and goes

    c. What does God want from people? (verse 6)

    To be faithful to God and come to know God

2. Read Hosea 13:4.

    Who does God say that He is?

    The only God, the God who brought you forth from Egypt, the only God who can save you

SESSION 13 ACTIVITY WORKSHEET – PAGE 2 **TEACHER'S COPY**

3. Read Hosea 2:19-23.

   a. What does God promise to give to Israel in verses 19-20?
   Justice, fairness, love, kindness, and faithfulness

   b. What are the people Israel to answer in response to God's promises? (verse 23)
   "You are our God."

4. Read Hosea 11:1-9.

   a. To what does the Lord compare His love for Israel? (verse 1)
   As a father loves a son

   b. How did Israel respond to God's love? (verse 2)
   They rebelled, worshiped false gods.

   c. What does God promise in verses 8-9?
   God will not give up on them or let them go. He promises not to destroy them or stay angry long.

JOURNEY OF HOPE

SESSION 14

Amos: Do the Right Thing

OBJECTIVE

Students will discover and apply to their own lives the prophetic message of Amos.

READER

Chapter 14: Promise of Restoration

LESSON PLAN

PRAYER

Opening prayer

REVIEW

Ask for volunteers to show and explain their Acrostic from Session 13 describing God's love. Next ask:

1. Why are we studying the prophets? What can we learn from them?

2. Of the prophets we've studied so far, which prophet's message do you think most needs to be heard by people today? Why?

OBJECTIVE

Explain that in today's session students will read, discuss, and reflect on important prophetic messages from another famous Old Testament prophet, Amos.

ACTIVITY

1. As a class, read the introduction to the book of Amos in the Bible.

2. Then direct students to complete the Activity worksheet for this session. (Students may work alone or with a partner.) Allow 10 minutes to complete the worksheet.)

3. Call the class back as a large group to discuss students' findings.

CONNECTION

After discussing the Activity worksheet, have students take the following notes:

- Amos was a shepherd from the town of Tekoa. Amos discovered that God's purpose for his life was to speak God's message to the sinful people of Israel.

- Amos' one-item agenda is the "Righteousness of God:" God always does the right thing and expects us to do likewise.

- According to Amos, God's righteousness is real in our lives only when we have a personal relationship with the Lord. (Amos 5:4) Our God has "known and cared for" us. (Amos 3:2) We are intimately connected to God. And in response, we are called to know the Lord personally as His friend and servant.

- Amos reminds us of all God has done in the past to free His people from enslavement and bring the people together as the family of God. (The Exodus from Egypt: freedom from sin and evil)

- Amos teaches us that in order to develop a personal relationship with God that we must:

    Repent (turn away from) our sins.

    Do what is right.

- Then "the Lord God Almighty really will stay with you." (Amos 5:14)

REFLECTION

Distribute Reflection Questions worksheet. Give time to complete in class or assign for homework.

SESSION 14 AMOS: DO THE RIGHT THING
ACTIVITY WORKSHEET

Name_____

Directions: Answer the questions below by reading the listed passages from the Old Testament book of Amos.

1. What job did Amos have? (Amos 1:1)

2. Where was he from? (Amos 1:1)

3. How did Amos discover God's purpose for his life? (Amos 7:15)

4. According to Amos 3:3-8, what is the work of a prophet?

5. What sins were the people committing that Amos spoke out about?

Amos 2:4

Amos 2:6-8

Amos 3:10

Amos 5:10-12

Amos 8:4-6

SESSION 14 ACTIVITY WORKSHEET – PAGE 2

6. Name current examples of these same types of sins in today's world.

7. What makes the people's sins so terrible to the Lord? (Amos 3:1-2)

8. What should the people be doing?

9. What will happen to the people if they do not change their ways?
Amos 2:6

Amos 9:9

SESSION 14 AMOS: DO THE RIGHT THING
ACTIVITY WORKSHEET

Teacher's Copy

Directions: Answer the questions below by reading the listed passages from the Old Testament book of Amos.

1. What job did Amos have? (Amos 1:1)

Shepherd

2. Where was he from? (Amos 1:1)

Tekoa

3. How did Amos discover God's purpose for his life? (Amos 7:15)

God came to him while he was herding sheep and instructed him to go preach to the people of Israel.

4. According to Amos 3:3-8, what is the work of a prophet?

To reveal God's plan and proclaim God's message

5. What sins were the people committing that Amos spoke out about?

Amos 2:4

Rejecting God's teachings, refusing to obey God, worshiping false gods

Amos 2:6-8

Selling the poor into slavery, treating the poor badly

Amos 3:10

Not knowing how to do right, committing violence, robbery

Amos 5:10-12

Hating judges and honesty, abusing the poor, cheating, taking bribes

Amos 8:4-6

Not helping the needy, cheating, being dishonest, practicing slavery

SESSION 14 ACTIVITY WORKSHEET – PAGE 2 **TEACHER'S COPY**

6. Name current examples of these same types of sins in today's world.

Open-ended

7. What makes the people's sins so terrible to the Lord? (Amos 3:1-2)

Because they are God's chosen people

8. What should the people be doing?

Living out the Covenant – being God's people by living according to God's ways

9. What will happen to the people if they do not change their ways?

Amos 2:6

They will be punished.

Amos 9:9

They will be scattered and separated – especially separated from God.

Reflection Questions

Directions: Review your notes and your Session 14 Activity worksheet to help you answer the questions below.

1. What is the central message (one-item agenda) of Amos' prophecy?

2. According to Amos, what must we do in order to develop a personal relationship with God?

3. What is the difference between knowing about God and knowing God? Explain.

4. According to Amos 5:14, the Lord will really be on our side when we do what?

SESSION 14 HOMEWORK – PAGE 2

5. Amos reminds us of all God has done in the past to free us from enslavement and to bring us together as the family of God. Describe something God has done in your past to free you from something that enslaved you.

6. The word "repent" means literally "to turn away from." List below the negative attitudes or behaviors you need to turn away from.

7. Amos tells us to "make it your aim to do what is right." (5:14) List 10 specific "right" things you will do in the next few days. (i.e., be honest with my parents, smile at new kids, say thank you more often, etc.)

SESSION 14 — AMOS: DO THE RIGHT THING
HOMEWORK

TEACHER'S COPY

Reflection Questions

Directions: Review your notes and your Session 14 Activity worksheet to help you answer the questions below.

1. What is the central message (one-item agenda) of Amos' prophecy?

The righteousness of God

2. According to Amos, what must we do in order to develop a personal relationship with God?

Repent from sin and do what is right.

3. What is the difference between knowing about God and knowing God? Explain.

Knowing about God is just information. Knowing God implies that I've allowed this information about God and from God to transform and affect my daily life.

4. According to Amos 5:14, the Lord will really be on our side when we do what?

Stop doing wrong and start doing right.

SESSION 14 HOMEWORK – PAGE 2   **TEACHER'S COPY**

5. Amos reminds us of all God has done in the past to free us from enslavement and to bring us together as the family of God. Describe something God has done in your past to free you from something that enslaved you.

Open-ended

6. The word "repent" means literally "to turn away from." List below the negative attitudes or behaviors you need to turn away from.

Open-ended

7. Amos tells us to "make it your aim to do what is right." (5:14) List 10 specific "right" things you will do in the next few days. (i.e., be honest with my parents, smile at new kids, say thank you more often, etc.)

Open-ended

JOURNEY OF HOPE

SESSION 15

Malachi: Respect Me by What You Do

LESSON PLAN

OBJECTIVE

Students will read, discuss, and reflect on the prophetic message of Malachi.

READER

Chapter 15: Being Faithful in Bad Times

PRAYER

Opening prayer

REVIEW

Discuss the following questions:

What is a prophet?

Why are we studying prophets?

OBJECTIVE

State as described at left.

ACTIVITY

1. As a class, read the introduction and the book of Malachi. A suggested technique for group reading is "Round Robin." (Instructions follow.)

2. Have students arrange desks so that they can hear and see one another well.

145

3. Instruct everyone to open Bible to the book of Malachi. Explain that they will take turns reading from Malachi using the following methods:

   - Teacher will call on someone. That person must read at least one sentence, but no more than one paragraph.

   - Whenever finished, that person calls on another student to read. Reader 2 may have to begin reading in the middle of a word, the middle of a sentence, or the middle of a paragraph – wherever Reader 1 decides.

   - The reading continues to be passed around until completed. All must be listening closely and reading along since no one knows exactly when he or she will be called on.

4. The teacher may want to establish and administer consequences for those not on task or not paying attention when called on.

5. After reading Malachi, distribute the Activity worksheet for this session. Students may work alone or with a partner to complete. Allow 10-15 minutes to complete.

6. When all have completed worksheets, discuss their answers.

CONNECTION

After discussing the Activity worksheet, have students take the following notes:

- The book of Malachi was written about 400 years before Jesus' birth. The people of Malachi's time had a beautifully rebuilt Temple to worship God in, but they had become insincere in their worship of God and sinful in their behavior toward God.

- Malachi reminds the people of God's ever-present love for them and His covenant promises of life and well-being. In return, God expects people to respect Him by what we do. We can show that respect by:

Teaching what is right.

　　　Living according to God's ways (Ten Commandments).

　　　Leading others away from sin by being good role models.

- Instead of the covenant behaviors God desired, the people of Malachi's time were disrespectful of God by:

　　　Offering unacceptable sacrifices (cheating God)

　　　Leading others to do wrong (bad examples)

　　　Questioning God's love for them

　　　Believing it's useless to serve God and useless to repent

　　　Giving false testimony (lying)

　　　Cheating – employers cheating employees, spouses cheating on one another

　　　Taking advantage of widows, orphans, and foreigners

　　　Envying the proud and the evil-doers

- The main message of Malachi is to respect God by what we do, especially in worship!

REFLECTION

Complete the Reflection Questions worksheet for homework.

SESSION 15
MALACHI: RESPECT ME BY WHAT YOU DO
ACTIVITY WORKSHEET

Name_____

Directions: After reading the book of Malachi, answer the following questions.

1. What does the Lord say to His people in Malachi 1:2? How do the people respond?

2. Read Malachi 1:6-9. How are the people disrespectful toward God?

3. Read Malachi 1:10-14.

   a. Who else respects and praises God?

   b. How do they show respect to God?

   c. How are the people Israel being disrespectful of God?

   d. How does God feel about such disrespect?

4. Read Malachi 2:4-8.

   a. What did God promise in His covenant agreement with Levi?

   b. How did Levi show respect for God?

© 2001 by Father Flanagan's Boys' Home.

JOURNEY OF HOPE

SESSION 15 ACTIVITY WORKSHEET – PAGE 2

    c. What is the duty of the priests?

    d. How have the priests, the descendants of Levi, broken the covenant agreement?

5. List the three important questions Malachi asks in Chapter 2:10.

6. Read the following passages and write how the people sinned against God.
    a. Malachi 2:11

    b. Malachi 2:13-16

    c. Malachi 2:17

    d. Malachi 3:5

SESSION 15 ACTIVITY WORKSHEET – PAGE 3

7. What terrible things had the people said about God?

    a.   Malachi 3:14

    b.   Malachi 3:15

8. What kind of behavior does God want from His people?

    a.   Malachi 2:2

    b.   Malachi 3:6-10

    c.   Malachi 2:15-16

    d.   Malachi 2:6

9. How will God show His mercy to those who do repent and come back to God?

    a.   Malachi 3:16-18

    b.   Malachi 4:2-3

JOURNEY OF HOPE

SESSION 15 MALACHI: RESPECT ME BY WHAT YOU DO

ACTIVITY WORKSHEET

TEACHER'S COPY

Directions: After reading the book of Malachi, answer the following questions.

1. What does the Lord say to His people in Malachi 1:2? How do the people respond?

   The Lord proclaims his love for Israel. The people respond by asking God to describe the ways he has loved them.

2. Read Malachi 1:6-9. How are the people disrespectful toward God?

   By making worthless sacrifices and offerings to God

3. Read Malachi 1:10-14.

   a. Who else respects and praises God?

   Every nation on earth

   b. How do they show respect to God?

   Offer proper sacrifices

   c. How are the people Israel being disrespectful of God?

   Offering worthless and stolen sacrifices; making vulgar signs at God

   d. How does God feel about such disrespect?

   God is displeased, embarrassed, angry, will punish.

4. Read Malachi 2:4-8.

   a. What did God promise in His covenant agreement with Levi?

   Gave Levi a full life

   b. How did Levi show respect for God?

   Taught the truth, never lied, led people to repent, obeyed God, and lived right

SESSION 15 ACTIVITY WORKSHEET – PAGE 2 **TEACHER'S COPY**

    c. What is the duty of the priests?

       To spread knowledge of God, teach, speak for the Lord

    d. How have the priests, the descendants of Levi, broken the covenant agreement?

       They turned their backs on God and led others to sin.

5. List the three important questions Malachi asks in Chapter 2:10.

    1. *Don't you know that we all have God as our Father?*

    2. *Didn't God create each of us?*

    3. *Why do you cheat each other by breaking the agreement God made with your ancestors?*

6. Read the following passages and write how the people sinned against God.

    a. Malachi 2:11

       Unfaithful to God disgraced the temple, worshiped other gods

    b. Malachi 2:13-16

       Unfaithful to spouses

    c. Malachi 2:17

       Rationalized their sin by thinking and saying that God is pleased with evil and doesn't care about justice

    d. Malachi 3:5

       Practiced witchcraft, cheated on spouses, lied in court, robbed workers of pay, mistreated widows and orphans, stole, refused to respect God

SESSION 15 ACTIVITY WORKSHEET – PAGE 3 **TEACHER'S COPY**

7. What terrible things had the people said about God?

    a. Malachi 3:14

    It's foolish to serve and obey the Lord.

    b. Malachi 3:15

    Arrogant people are happy. Those who do wrong are successful. Test God and see what you can get away with.

8. What kind of behavior does God want from His people?

    a. Malachi 2:2

    Honor God's name.

    b. Malachi 3:6-10

    Return to God by offering acceptable sacrifices.

    c. Malachi 2:15-16

    Become one with your spouse, have children, and lead them to be God's people.

    d. Malachi 2:6

    Teach the truth, never lie, lead others to repent, obey God, live right.

9. How will God show His mercy to those who do repent and come back to God?

    a. Malachi 3:16-18

    God will protect them and be just toward them.

    b. Malachi 4:2-3

    The just will be triumphant over evil people.

SESSION 15 MALACHI: RESPECT ME BY WHAT YOU DO
HOMEWORK

Name_____

Reflection Questions

Directions: Review the book of Malachi and your notes from this session to help you answer the questions below.

1. What is the main message of the prophet Malachi?

2. List five ways the people of Malachi's time were disrespectful and sinful toward God.

   a.

   b.

   c.

   d.

   e.

3. List ten specific examples of how people today are disrespectful and sinful toward God.

4. List the three covenant behaviors that God desires of people.

   a.

   b.

   c.

SESSION 15 HOMEWORK – PAGE 2

5. For each of the three covenant behaviors God desires, list three specific examples of how you could live out that covenant behavior.

   a. Three ways I can live out covenant behavior #1 are:

      1.

      2.

      3.

   b. Three ways I can live out covenant behavior #2 are:

      1.

      2.

      3.

   c. Three ways I can live out covenant behavior #3 are:

      1.

      2.

      3.

6. What two things does the Lord promise if we live according to His covenant?

   a.

   b.

SESSION **15** MALACHI: RESPECT ME BY WHAT YOU DO
HOMEWORK

Teacher's Copy

Reflection Questions

Directions: Review the book of Malachi and your notes from this session to help you answer the questions below.

1. What is the main message of the prophet Malachi?

   Respect God by what we do, especially in worship.

2. List five ways the people of Malachi's time were disrespectful and sinful toward God.
   a. *Unfaithful to spouses*
   b. *Offered unacceptable sacrifices*
   c. *Led others to sin*
   d. *Lied and cheated*
   e. *Worshiped false gods*

3. List ten specific examples of how people today are disrespectful and sinful toward God.

   Open-ended

4. List the three covenant behaviors that God desires of people.
   a. *Teach what is right.*
   b. *Live according to God's ways.*
   c. *Lead others away from sin by being a good role model.*

SESSION 15 HOMEWORK – PAGE 2   **TEACHER'S COPY**

5. For each of the three covenant behaviors God desires, list three specific examples of how you could live out that covenant behavior.

    a. Three ways I can live out covenant behavior #1 are:

       1. *Open-ended*

       2.

       3.

    b. Three ways I can live out covenant behavior #2 are:

       1. *Open-ended*

       2.

       3.

    c. Three ways I can live out covenant behavior #3 are:

       1. *Open-ended*

       2.

       3.

6. What two things does the Lord promise if we live according to His covenant?

    a. *He will be our God.*

    b. *We will be His people.*

JOURNEY OF HOPE

SESSION 16

Malachi: Worship God Sincerely

LESSON PLAN

OBJECTIVE

Enable students to apply Malachi's main message – "Respect God by what you do" – to their behavior and attitudes toward public worship.

READER

Chapter 16: Worship God Sincerely

PRAYER

Opening prayer

REVIEW

Begin this session by inviting students to share their answers from the last session's Reflection Questions homework.

OBJECTIVE

Explain that today's session is designed to help students apply Malachi's main message, "Respect God by what you do," to how they participate in public worship of God.

ACTIVITY

Continue by explaining: *"In order to get the most out of today's session, there are two words we need to clearly understand. The following activity will help us begin to come to a deeper understanding of the words 'worship' and 'sincere.'"*

1. Divide students into teams of two or three.

2. Give each team a piece of paper and pen. Instruct each team to divide its paper into two columns. Title one column "worship" and the other "sincere."

3. Explain that you are going to display on the overhead (or write on the board) words or phrases that define or describe either "worship" or "sincere." Their task is to, as a team, decide in which column to write the word or phrase displayed. The team with the most correct answers at the end will be awarded a teacher-designated positive consequence (an "A", bonus points, positive phone call home, etc.).

4. Display words/phrases one at a time. Allow about 30 seconds for teams to discuss and write. Then move on to next word/phrase. (See attached Word List for teacher use.)

5. After about 5-7 minutes, stop activity. Instruct teams to write their names at the top of the page and then to switch papers with another team. Teacher reads correct answers aloud while students correct one another's papers. Teacher collects papers for grading/recording.

CONNECTION

Distribute the handout for this session. Summarize by having students read aloud the following notes. Instruct them to keep these notes in their binders.

- To worship God means to publicly or privately offer our praise, prayers, respect for, and dedication to God. The noun "worship" refers to a public church service.

- To be sincere means you are genuine, authentic, or real. A sincere person is honest, straightforward, and serious.

- Malachi's message is to honor God by what we do. It is a plea for sincere worship of God.

- Some ways we can be more sincere in our public worship of God are:
  - Before the service begins, sit or kneel and quietly greet the Lord. Say a prayer or two. Ask God to open your mind and heart to Him so that you can get closer to God and learn something new about God or yourself today.
  - While waiting for the service to begin, read over the readings, again asking God to give you insight into His word.
  - Listen closely to the words of Scripture, the words of the sermon, the words of the songs that are sung. Pick out one main idea from each to think and pray about, and apply to your life.
  - Pray sincerely. Open your heart to God and to your brothers and sisters in prayer. Ask God for the strength to repent your sins and to be more sincere in all your relationships.
  - Offer to God the best you have to give. Give God the best of yourself: your gifts and talents and hopes and dreams. Ask God to help you use these wisely for the good of all. (Give to God the best you have, and the best will come back to you.)

REFLECTION

Distribute Reflection Questions worksheet for this session. Allow time to complete or assign for homework.

SESSION 16 — MALACHI: WORSHIP GOD SINCERELY
WORD LIST

TEACHER'S COPY

WORSHIP	SINCERE
adore	genuine
reverence	honest
venerate	real
praise	true
love	heartfelt
show affection	candid
public prayer	straightforward
honor	open
show respect for	truthful
church service	wholehearted
religious devotion	authentic
admire	serious

SESSION 16 — MALACHI: WORSHIP GOD SINCERELY
HANDOUT

Worship God Sincerely

To worship God means to publicly or privately offer our praise, prayers, respect for and dedication to God. The noun "worship" refers to a public church service.

To be sincere means you are genuine, authentic, or real. A sincere person is honest, straightforward, and serious.

Malachi's message is to honor God by what we do. It is a plea for sincere worship of God.

Some ways we can be more sincere in our public worship of God are:

- Before the service begins, sit or kneel and quietly greet the Lord. Say a prayer or two. Ask God to open your mind and heart to Him so that you can get closer to God and learn something new about God or yourself today.

- While waiting for the service to begin, read over the readings, again asking God to give you insight into His word.

- Listen closely to the words of Scripture, the words of the sermon, the words of the songs that are sung. Pick out one main idea from each to think and pray about, and apply to your life.

- Pray sincerely. Open your heart to God and to your brothers and sisters in prayer. Ask God for the strength to repent your sins and to be more sincere in all your relationships.

- Offer to God the best you have to give. Give God the best of yourself: your gifts and talents and hopes and dreams. Ask God to help you use these wisely for the good of all. (Give to God the best you have and the best will come back to you.)

- Participate by:
  Singing with enthusiasm
  Reading with involvement
  Listening in order to learn

SESSION 16 MALACHI: WORSHIP GOD SINCERELY
ACTIVITY WORKSHEET

Name_____

Reflection Questions

Directions: Review your notes and handout from today's class to help you answer the questions below.

1. According to your notes, what is "worship?"

2. According to your notes, what does it mean to be "sincere?"

3. How sincere are you, usually, when you worship God? Explain why.

SESSION 16 ACTIVITY WORKSHEET – PAGE 2

4. What could you do to show more sincerity to God when you worship? Give five specific examples.

5. What would help you be more sincere in worshiping God? Explain.

6. Why do you think God wants us to be sincere in our worship of Him? Explain.

SESSION 16 MALACHI: WORSHIP GOD SINCERELY

TEACHER'S COPY

ACTIVITY WORKSHEET

Reflection Questions

Directions: Review your notes and handout from today's class to help you answer the questions below.

1. According to your notes, what is "worship?"

Offering our praise, prayers, respect for, and dedication to God

2. According to your notes, what does it mean to be "sincere?"

Being genuine, authentic, real, honest, straightforward, and serious

3. How sincere are you, usually, when you worship God? Explain why.

Open-ended

SESSION 16 ACTIVITY WORKSHEET – PAGE 2 **TEACHER'S COPY**

4. What could you do to show more sincerity to God when you worship? Give five specific examples.

Open-ended

5. What would help you be more sincere in worshiping God? Explain.

Open-ended

6. Why do you think God wants us to be sincere in our worship of Him? Explain.

Open-ended

JOURNEY OF HOPE

SESSION 17

Jonah: Prophetic Parable about God's Forgiveness

LESSON PLAN

OBJECTIVE

Students will read the book of Jonah and discover the message of this prophetic parable.

READER

Chapter 17: Do Not Wish Evil

NOTE TO THE TEACHER

Please refrain from discussing with students whether or not the Jonah story really happened or is "just a story." Teach that it is a prophetic parable with an important message about the forgiveness and mercy of God. See information under "Activity" for more details.

PRAYER

Opening prayer

REVIEW

Discuss the following questions to help students recall the purpose of studying the prophets:

1. Why do we study the prophets?
   Because they can inspire us and we can learn from their message and apply it to our own lives

2. Each prophet has a specific purpose and message given by God. Name a prophet we've studied so far and briefly explain his purpose/message.

3. Each prophet faced difficult challenges in doing God's will. Describe one prophet's challenges and what happened when he did God's will.

OBJECTIVE

Explain: *"In this session, we will read the prophetic book of Jonah in order to discover the message God gave Jonah to proclaim and how this message applies to our lives today."*

ACTIVITY

1. Explain that *"in order to get the most out of reading and discussing the book of Jonah, we need to understand a few very important points about this book."* Have students take the following notes:

   - The book of Jonah is different from other prophetic books. Unlike other prophetic books, the book of Jonah is not a biography of the life of a prophet.

   - The book of Jonah is a prophetic parable. A parable is a simple story told to convey a deeper spiritual meaning.

   - The book of Jonah is a story about the forgiveness and mercy of God. Even God's ministers and prophets sometimes don't understand the depths of God's mercy and kindness.

2. Direct students to read the book of Jonah. This can be done in pairs or as a large group.

3. After reading is completed, distribute the Activity worksheet for this session. Allow students time to complete.

4. Discuss their responses to the worksheet.

CONNECTION

After discussing the Activity worksheet, make the following connections for the students. Have students write these as notes.

- God saved Jonah's life by forgiving him and giving him a second chance. Jonah "rose" to new life through this forgiveness. This is often referred to as the "Sign of Jonah."

- God's forgiveness of Jonah is a sign to us all – it points to the kinds of forgiveness and mercy that are available to all of us from God.

- God's forgiveness is even for our enemies. (Ninevah was an enemy of the Hebrews.)

- Even some of God's ministers, like the prophet Jonah, sometimes don't understand and don't accept the fullness of God's kindness and mercy.

REFLECTION/HOMEWORK

Distribute the Reflection Questions worksheet. Instruct students to complete now or for homework.

SESSION 17 — JONAH: PROPHETIC PARABLE
ACTIVITY WORKSHEET

Name_____

Directions: After reading the book of Jonah, answer the following questions.

1. What instruction did God give Jonah? (Jonah 1:2)

2. Instead of following God's instructions, what did Jonah do? (Jonah 1:3)

3. Why did Jonah disobey God's instruction? (introduction)

4. What happened to the ship Jonah was sailing on? (Jonah 1:4-5)

5. What was Jonah's solution for calming the storm? (Jonah 1:12)

6. What did the sailors do first, instead of throwing Jonah overboard? (Jonah 1:13)

© 2001 by Father Flanagan's Boys' Home.

JOURNEY OF HOPE

SESSION 17 ACTIVITY WORKSHEET – PAGE 2

7. What did the sailors finally do with Jonah? (Jonah 1:15)

8. What happened to Jonah once he was thrown overboard? (Jonah 1:17)

9. How long was Jonah inside the fish? (Jonah 1:17)

10. What did Jonah do while inside the fish? (Jonah 2:1)

11. What was the general theme of Jonah's prayers? (Jonah 2:2-9)

12. What happened to Jonah in Jonah 2:10?

SESSION 17 ACTIVITY WORKSHEET – PAGE 3

13. What does Jonah do when God asks him for the second time to go and preach to Nineveh? (Jonah 3:1-4)

14. How did the people of Nineveh respond to God's message spoken through Jonah? (Jonah 3:5)

15. What proclamation did the King of Nineveh make in Jonah 3:6-9?

16. How did God respond to their repentance? (Jonah 3:10)

17. How did Jonah feel about God's mercy toward Nineveh? Why? (Jonah 4)

18. What can we learn about God from this story? Explain.

SESSION 17 JONAH: PROPHETIC PARABLE
ACTIVITY WORKSHEET

TEACHER'S COPY

Directions: After reading the book of Jonah, answer the following questions.

1. What instruction did God give Jonah in Jonah 1:2?
   Go to Nineveh and preach to the people about their sinfulness.

2. Instead of following God's instructions, what did Jonah do? (Jonah 1:3)
   He got on a ship headed for Spain to try to escape from God's call.

3. Why did Jonah disobey God's instruction? (introduction)
   Jonah wanted Ninevah to be destroyed, not saved.

4. What happened to the ship Jonah was sailing on? (Jonah 1:4-5)
   It came upon a bad storm that threatened to destroy the ship.

5. What was Jonah's solution for calming the storm? (Jonah 1:12)
   Jonah told the sailors to throw him into the sea.

6. What did the sailors do first, instead of throwing Jonah overboard? (Jonah 1:13)
   They tried to row ashore instead.

SESSION 17 ACTIVITY WORKSHEET – PAGE 2   **TEACHER'S COPY**

7. What did the sailors finally do with Jonah? (Jonah 1:15)

They threw him overboard.

8. What happened to Jonah once he was thrown overboard? (Jonah 1:17)

He was swallowed by a big fish.

9. How long was Jonah inside the fish? (Jonah 1:17)

Three days and nights

10. What did Jonah do while inside the fish? (Jonah 2:1)

He prayed to God.

11. What was the general theme of Jonah's prayers? (Jonah 2:2-9)

Sorrow, repentance, remembering and thanking God for all the times God had rescued him

12. What happened to Jonah in Jonah 2:10?

By God's command, the fish vomited Jonah onto the shore.

SESSION 17 ACTIVITY WORKSHEET – PAGE 3 **TEACHER'S COPY**

13. What does Jonah do when God asks him for the second time to go and preach to Nineveh? (Jonah 3:1-4)

Jonah obeyed.

14. How did the people of Nineveh respond to God's message spoken through Jonah? (Jonah 3:5)

They believed God's message, repented, fasted, made amends.

15. What proclamation did the King of Nineveh make in Jonah 3:6-9?

That all should repent, pray to God, stop sinfulness and cruelty

16. How did God respond to their repentance? (Jonah 3:10)

With pity, and He did not destroy them.

17. How did Jonah feel about God's mercy toward Nineveh? Why? (Jonah 4)

He was upset and angry because his enemies, the people of Ninevah, were receiving mercy and forgiveness from God, two things that Jonah could not give them.

18. What can we learn about God from this story? Explain.

God's forgiveness is for everyone who repents; God's ability to forgive surpasses our own.

SESSION 17 — JONAH: PROPHETIC PARABLE
HOMEWORK

Name_____

Reflection Questions

Directions: Answer the following questions based on your study and discussion of the book of Jonah.

1. Something I learned from reading and discussing the book of Jonah is...

2. I am like/not like Jonah because...

3. The deeper spiritual meaning of the book of Jonah is...

SESSION 17 HOMEWORK – PAGE 2

4. A parable is...

5. Who is God's mercy and kindness for? Explain.

6. In what areas of your life do you most need God's mercy? Why?

7. How will you go about repenting in this area of your life (changing your ways and returning to God's ways)? Explain.

SESSION 17 — JONAH: PROPHETIC PARABLE
HOMEWORK

TEACHER'S COPY

Reflection Questions

Directions: Answer the following questions based on your study and discussion of the book of Jonah.

1. Something I learned from reading and discussing the book of Jonah is...

Open-ended

2. I am like/not like Jonah because...

Open-ended

3. The deeper spiritual meaning of the book of Jonah is...

that God's forgiveness is open to all who repent and that it is a second chance at a new life with God.

SESSION 17 HOMEWORK – PAGE 2   **TEACHER'S COPY**

4. A parable is...

a simple story told to convey a deeper spiritual message.

5. Who is God's mercy and kindness for? Explain.

For everyone who repents

6. In what areas of your life do you most need God's mercy? Why?

Open-ended

7. How will you go about repenting in this area of your life (changing your ways and returning to God's ways)? Explain.

Open-ended

JOURNEY OF HOPE
SESSION 18

Jonah: Sin, Consequences, and Repentance

OBJECTIVE

Students will discover and apply to their own lives what the book of Jonah can teach us about sin, consequences, and repentance.

READER

Chapter 18: Sin and Repentance

LESSON PLAN

PRAYER

Opening prayer

REVIEW

Discuss the student's responses to the Reflection Questions from the previous session.

OBJECTIVE

State as described at left.

ACTIVITY

Explain: *"Even though the book of Jonah is short, it is packed with powerful lessons for us. Today's activity will help you review and apply to your own lives some important lessons we can learn from Jonah about sin, the consequences of our sin, our need to repent of our sinful ways, and how to repent."*

1. Distribute and explain the Activity worksheet. This activity may be completed in small groups, pairs, or as individuals.

187

2. Allow time to complete the worksheet.

3. Present stories to the whole group.

CONNECTION

After each small group has presented, have students take the following notes:

- The Jonah story reminds us that refusing and running away from God is sin. When we sin, we will suffer consequences. Often, like the sailors on Jonah's ship, those around us will also suffer because of our sin.

- The people of Nineveh put on sackcloth, sat in ashes, and fasted as public signs of repenting (returning to God's ways). We, too, need to publicly and privately show signs of our repentance when we sin.

REFLECTION/HOMEWORK

Distribute and explain Reflection Questions as homework.

SESSION 18
JONAH: SIN, CONSEQUENCES, AND REPENTANCE
ACTIVITY WORKSHEET

Name_____

PART 1

Directions: Review your notes and worksheets from the last session on Jonah. Then answer the following questions.

1. What did God ask Jonah to do?

2. How did Jonah disobey God?

3. What were the consequences of Jonah's disobedience?

4. How did Jonah's disobedience affect others (the sailors and the captain)?

5. How did Jonah spend his time while he was inside the fish?

6. How did Jonah's attitude change while inside the fish?

SESSION 18 ACTIVITY WORKSHEET – PAGE 2

7. How did Jonah respond the second time God asked him to go to Nineveh?

8. How did the people of Nineveh respond to Jonah's preaching?

9. How did God respond to Nineveh's repentance?

PART 2

Write your own modern day Jonah parable. Make sure to include the following in your parable:

1. Brief description of your main character, who his or her enemies are, and how God instructs your main character to go to those enemies to preach a message of repentance.

2. How your main character refuses to preach God's message and runs away.

3. The consequences your main character faces as a result of disobeying or refusing God and running away.

4. How your main character's sin affects others.

5. What happens to your main character that enables him or her to recognize his or her own sin, repent, and return to preach God's message.

6. How your character preaches repentance to his or her enemies.

7. How the enemies show repentance as a result of the preaching.

8. How God responds to their sincere repentance.

SESSION 18 JONAH: SIN, CONSEQUENCES, AND REPENTANCE **TEACHER'S COPY**

ACTIVITY WORKSHEET

PART 1

Directions: Review your notes and worksheets from the last session on Jonah. Then answer the following questions.

1. What did God ask Jonah to do?

   Go to Ninevah and preach about their need to repent.

2. How did Jonah disobey God?

   He ran away from God.

3. What were the consequences of Jonah's disobedience?

   He encountered a storm at sea and was swallowed by a large fish.

4. How did Jonah's disobedience affect others (the sailors and the captain)?

   Their lives were in danger because of Jonah's sin.

5. How did Jonah spend his time while he was inside the fish?

   Praying

6. How did Jonah's attitude change while inside the fish?

   He remembered God's faithfulness and love and became willing to do what God asked.

SESSION 18 ACTIVITY WORKSHEET – PAGE 2   **TEACHER'S COPY**

7. How did Jonah respond the second time God asked him to go to Nineveh?

He went and preached to Ninevah.

8. How did the people of Nineveh respond to Jonah's preaching?

They repented, prayed, and stopped sinning.

9. How did God respond to Nineveh's repentance?

He forgave them – did not destroy them.

PART 2

Write your own modern day Jonah parable. Make sure to include the following in your parable:

1. Brief description of your main character, who his or her enemies are, and how God instructs your main character to go to those enemies to preach a message of repentance.

2. How your main character refuses to preach God's message and runs away.

3. The consequences your main character faces as a result of disobeying or refusing God and running away.

4. How your main character's sin affects others.

5. What happens to your main character that enables him or her to recognize his or her own sin, repent, and return to preach God's message.

6. How your character preaches repentance to his or her enemies.

7. How the enemies show repentance as a result of the preaching.

8. How God responds to their sincere repentance.

SESSION 18 | JONAH: SIN, CONSEQUENCES, AND REPENTANCE
HOMEWORK

Name_____

Reflection Questions

Directions: List below 20 sins teens commonly commit. In the next column describe what that teen could do to show repentance to God and others.

Sinful Behaviors	Ways to Show Repentance
1.	1.
2.	2.
3.	3.
4.	4.
5.	5.
6.	6.
7.	7.
8.	8.
9.	9.
10.	10.

SESSION 18 HOMEWORK – PAGE 2

Sinful Behaviors	Ways to Show Repentance
11.	11.
12.	12.
13.	13.
14.	14.
15.	15.
16.	16.
17.	17.
18.	18.
19.	19.
20.	20.

SESSION 18 JONAH: SIN, CONSEQUENCES, AND REPENTANCE **TEACHER'S COPY**
HOMEWORK

Reflection Questions

Directions: List below 20 sins teens commonly commit. In the next column describe what that teen could do to show repentance to God and others.

Sinful Behaviors	Ways to Show Repentance
1. *Gossiping about others*	1. *Refusing to spread gossip anymore. Apologizing to those you gossiped about.*
2. *Lying*	2. *Asking forgiveness and making amends to those lied to. Being honest in the future.*
3. *Disobeying parents*	3. *Seeking forgiveness from God and parents. Learning how to follow parents' instructions.*
4.	4.
5.	5.
6.	6.
7.	7.
8.	8.
9.	9.
10.	10.

SESSION 18 HOMEWORK – PAGE 2   **TEACHER'S COPY**

Sinful Behaviors	Ways to Show Repentance
11.	11.
12.	12.
13.	13.
14.	14.
15.	15.
16.	16.
17.	17.
18.	18.
19.	19.
20.	20.

JOURNEY OF HOPE
SESSION 19

The Sign of Jonah

LESSON PLAN

OBJECTIVE

Enable students to identify and reflect on the "Sign of Jonah," the cyclic process of the Paschal mystery.

READER

Chapter 19: The Sign of Jonah

PRAYER

Opening prayer

REVIEW

Discuss the following questions:

1. What did God call Jonah to do?
   Preach repentance to his enemies, Nineveh

2. How did Jonah respond to God's call?
   Ran away, refused

3. What were the consequences of running away and refusing God?
   Being swallowed by a fish

4. How did the time spent in the fish change Jonah?
   Asked God's forgiveness, repented, became willing to obey God

OBJECTIVE

Explain that today's session is going to help students learn more about this life-changing event of Jonah's and reflect on what this event, often called the Sign of Jonah, can teach them about their own journey of faith with God.

ACTIVITY

1. Have a volunteer read aloud Matthew 12:38-42.

2. Then discuss the following questions. (This activity could be done in pairs – reading the Scripture and answering the questions on paper, then discussing as a large group.)

    a. In verse 39, what is the only miracle Jesus says he will give?
    The miracle of Jonah

    b. What is the miracle of Jonah?
    The change God brought about in Jonah during the three days and nights in the fish. These three days remind us of the three days and nights of Jesus' death before His resurrection.

    c. What do you think Jesus means when He says in verse 41, "There is something here greater than Jonah"?
    The three days Jonah spent in the fish were a sign of something more – a symbol of a deeper spiritual reality.

CONNECTION

Have the students take the following notes on the Sign of Jonah:

- The Sign of Jonah is a term that refers to the change God brought about in Jonah through a three-day experience. It reminds us of the change God brings about in all believers through Jesus Christ's three-day passion, death, and resurrection.

- Jesus Christ's three-day experience involved death, resurrection, and new life.

- There are three elements to the Sign of Jonah. These three elements are experienced by all believers as they grow into a new life in Christ. These elements are a sign of God at work in our lives.

  The three elements are:

  1. **Dying** to old self, to old way of life, to sinfulness through…
  2. **Repentance**, turning away from sin and turning back to God, which brings…
  3. **Joy** in God's forgiveness, in new life and freedom from the trappings of a sinful life.

REFLECTION

Distribute and explain the Reflection Questions worksheet for this session. Read aloud together Part 1 of the Reflection Questions. Check for understanding. Explain Part 2 and then give time to complete or assign for homework.

SESSION 19: THE SIGN OF JONAH
ACTIVITY WORKSHEET

Name_____

Reflection Questions

Directions: Carefully and reflectively read over the explanation of the Three Elements of the Sign of Jonah in Part 1. Then answer the questions in Part 2.

PART 1: Three Elements of the Sign of Jonah

There are three elements of the Sign of Jonah. These elements are experienced by all believers as we grow in relationship with God and others. These elements are a sign of God at work in our lives.

1. **Dying – A time of death, loss, or great suffering**

   Often it is a time of darkness, grief, sadness, and even depression. It is like the three days of darkness Jonah spent inside the belly of the fish. Jonah's experience can teach us about how to handle these times of darkness. Jonah's experience teaches us that these dark times can become times of waiting for God, working on our relationship with God, and watching for signs of God at work in our lives. Jonah teaches us that in the dark times of our lives God will comfort us and bring forth something new in our lives.

2. **Repentance – A time of change**

   Repenting involves changing our minds, our attitudes, and our behaviors. It is a passing from old ways to new ways – from death to new life. During the "dying" times of our lives we need to be like Jonah; praying, inviting God to meet us in the darkness, asking God to change our minds and hearts. Seeking God's mercy and strength to change is the beginning of repentance.

3. **Joy – A time of experiencing God's steadfast love and mercy and rejoicing in it**

   This is a time of feeling "full of God." When we allow God to bring us from the darkness of dying to the light of His presence, we experience a deep sense of joy, wonder, and awe that moves us to be like Jonah, to thank God for His mercy, and to go forth to do God's will.

© 2001 by Father Flanagan's Boys' Home.

JOURNEY OF HOPE

SESSION 19 ACTIVITY WORKSHEET – PAGE 2

PART 2: Reflection Questions

Directions: Write or draw your responses to the three questions below. Use extra sheets of paper if needed.

1. Briefly describe a time in your life when you experienced great suffering, loss, or death. Did you allow God into this dark time of your life? Explain why or why not and what happened.

2. Briefly describe a time in your life when you changed or let go of old ways, repented, and began a new way of life. Was God a part of this? How?

3. Briefly describe a time in your life when you experienced joy or God's steadfast love and mercy? What happened?

JOURNEY OF HOPE

SESSION 20

Micah: Do Justice, Be Merciful, Humbly Obey God

OBJECTIVE

Students will discover and apply to their own lives the prophetic message of Micah.

READER

Chapter 20: Love God, Love Your Neighbor

LESSON PLAN

PRAYER

Opening prayer

REVIEW

Review the prophetic message of Jonah by discussing the Reflection Questions worksheet from the previous session.

OBJECTIVE

Explain: *"In today's session we will read the book of Micah, discover his one-item agenda, and apply his prophetic message to our own lives."*

ACTIVITY

Explain that the following activity and accompanying worksheet will help them learn more about the book of Micah.

1. Distribute and explain the Activity worksheet. Read aloud together the information at the top of the worksheet.

203

2. Divide the class into pairs to complete the worksheet. Allow 15-20 minutes to complete.

3. When the worksheets are completed, students should return to the large group to discuss their responses and correct the worksheets.

CONNECTION

After discussing the Activity worksheet, have the students take the following notes:

- Much of the book of Micah is written as if there is a trial. Micah speaks for the Lord as his prosecuting attorney.

- The mountains are the trial witnesses and the defendants are the people of Israel.

- Micah begins the trial by reminding the people of Israel of God's steadfast love for them throughout history.

- Micah continues by pointing out the sins of the people and how they have neglected the Lord by not responding to Him and by betraying His covenant.

- Micah concludes his case against Israel by stating his one-item agenda – the three things God does require of people:

  1. To do justice
  2. To be merciful
  3. To humbly obey God

- When we do these three things as God requires, we are showing that our faith is active and alive in these loving behaviors.

REFLECTION

Distribute the Reflection Questions worksheet. Explain that reflecting on and answering these questions will help students apply the message of Micah to their own lives. The worksheet may need to be completed as homework.

ACTION

If worksheet is completed during class, have students read Chapter 20 in the *Journey of Hope Reader*.

SUGGESTION FOR FOLLOW-UP ACTIVITY

Divide the class into small groups in which they will write and perform a contemporary play incorporating the three things God requires of people.

SESSION 20

MICAH: DO JUSTICE, BE MERCIFUL, HUMBLY OBEY GOD

ACTIVITY WORKSHEET

Name_____

Background Information on the book of Micah:
- Much of the book of Micah is written as if there is a trial.
- Micah is the Lord's prosecuting attorney.
- The defendants are the people of Israel.
- The mountains are the witnesses.

Direction: Read the following passages from Micah and answer the following questions to help you learn more about Micah, the Lord's case against Israel, and the fate of Israel.

1. Read Micah 1:1. Who gave Micah this message to preach?

2. Read Micah 2.
   a. What will happen to those who plan and do evil? (Micah 2:1-4)

   b. How do the people respond to Micah's preaching? (Micah 2:6-7)

   c. What does the Lord promise to those people of Israel who are left? (Micah 2:12-13)

3. Read Micah 3.
   a. What are Israel's rulers supposed to know? (Micah 3:1)

   b. What do Israel's rulers actually do? (Micah 3:2-3)

   c. What are the false prophets of Israel promising? (Micah 3:5)

   d. What will the consequences be for these false prophets? (Micah 3:6-7)

SESSION 20 ACTIVITY WORKSHEET – PAGE 2

    e. What does the Lord fill Micah with? (Micah 3:8)

    f. For what purpose did God give Micah a sense of justice and courage? (Micah 3:8)

4. Read Micah 6 through 7:7.

    a. Micah, the prosecuting attorney speaking for the Lord, begins the trial by reminding the people of what? (Micah 6:4-5)

    b. What sins are the people guilty of?
       Micah 6:10 –

       Micah 6:11 –

       Micah 6:12 –

       Micah 7:2 –

       Micah 7:3 –

    c. As a result of all their sins, Micah says the people are "in confusion." What are the consequences of their sins and confusion?
       Micah 7:5 -

       Micah 7:6 -

5. Read Micah 6:6-8. What three behaviors does the Lord want from the people Israel? (verse 8)

    a.

    b.

    c.

SESSION 20 ACTIVITY WORKSHEET – PAGE 3

6. Read Micah 4. The Lord wants to give his people peace. Life under the Lord's universal reign of peace will include:

Micah 4:2 – He will teach us _____.

We will _____.

Micah 4:3 – He will settle _____.

They will _____.

Nations will never again _____.

Micah 4:4 – Everyone will _____.

Micah 4:5 – We will always _____.

7. Read Micah 7:8-20.

a. Micah asks the Lord to do what for the people Israel?

Micah 7:14 – Be our _____.

Micah 7:15 – Work _____.

b. In verses 18-20, Micah describes the Lord as:

Micah 7:18 - No one is _____.

Micah 7:18 - You freely forgive _____.

Micah 7:18 - You don't stay _____ forever _____.

Micah 7:18 - You are pleased to be _____.

Micah 7:20 - You will keep your _____ and be _____.

SESSION 20 — MICAH: DO JUSTICE, BE MERCIFUL, HUMBLY OBEY GOD

ACTIVITY WORKSHEET

TEACHER'S COPY

Background Information on the book of Micah:
- Much of the book of Micah is written as if there is a trial.
- Micah is the Lord's prosecuting attorney.
- The defendants are the people of Israel.
- The mountains are the witnesses.

Direction: Read the following passages from Micah and answer the following questions to help you learn more about Micah, the Lord's case against Israel, and the fate of Israel.

1. Read Micah 1:1. Who gave Micah this message to preach?
   The Lord God

2. Read Micah 2.
   a. What will happen to those who plan and do evil? (Micah 2:1-4)
      Doomed, disgraced, ruined, and exiled from their homes

   b. How do the people respond to Micah's preaching? (Micah 2:6-7)
      They told Micah to stop, denied his message.

   c. What does the Lord promise to those people of Israel who are left? (Micah 2:12-13)
      To bring together those who survive

3. Read Micah 3.
   a. What are Israel's rulers supposed to know? (Micah 3:1)
      They're supposed to know right from wrong.

   b. What do Israel's rulers actually do? (Micah 3:2-3)
      They do evil.

   c. What are the false prophets of Israel promising? (Micah 3:5)
      False sense of security

   d. What will the consequences be for these false prophets? (Micah 3:6-7)
      They will be disgraced and will receive no messages from God.

SESSION 20 ACTIVITY WORKSHEET – PAGE 2 **TEACHER'S COPY**

    e. What does the Lord fill Micah with? (Micah 3:8)
With His power and Spirit

    f. For what purpose did God give Micah a sense of justice and courage? (Micah 3:8)
To speak to others about what is just and to tell Israel of their sinfulness

4. Read Micah 6 - 7:7.

    a. Micah, the prosecuting attorney speaking for the Lord, begins the trial by reminding the people of what? (Micah 6:4-5)
That God rescued them from slavery in Egypt and sent them leaders to lead them

    b. What sins are the people guilty of?
Micah 6:10 – *Stealing, cheating*

Micah 6:11 – *Cheating*

Micah 6:12 – *Violence, lying*

Micah 7:2 – *Being disloyal to God, not doing right*

Micah 7:3 – *Committing crimes, accepting bribes, cheating*

    c. As a result of all their sins, Micah says the people are "in confusion." What are the consequences of their sins and confusion?
Micah 7:5 – *Can't trust anyone, even best friends; have to be careful of what you say, even to loved ones*

Micah 7:6 – *Sons disrespecting fathers, daughters rebelling against mothers, family is enemy*

5. Read Micah 6:6-8. What three behaviors does the Lord want from the people Israel? (verse 8)

    a. *Do justice.*

    b. *Be merciful.*

    c. *Humbly obey God.*

SESSION 20 ACTIVITY WORKSHEET – PAGE 3   **TEACHER'S COPY**

6. Read Micah 4. The Lord wants to give his people peace. Life under the Lord's universal reign of peace will include:

Micah 4:2 – He will teach us ___*his law*___.

We will ___*obey him*___.

Micah 4:3 – He will settle ___*arguments*___.

They will ___*pound their swords into rakes and shovels*___.

Nations will never again ___*make war or attack one another*___.

Micah 4:4 – Everyone will ___*find rest, live in peace*___.

Micah 4:5 – We will always ___*follow…the Lord our God*___.

7. Read Micah 7:8-20.

a. Micah asks the Lord to do what for the people Israel?

Micah 7:14 – Be our ___*shepherd*___.

Micah 7:15 – Work ___*miracles*___.

b. In verses 18-20, Micah describes the Lord as:

Micah 7:18 - No one is ___*like you*___.

Micah 7:18 - You freely forgive ___*the sins of your people*___.

Micah 7:18 - You don't stay ___*angry*___ forever.

Micah 7:18 - You are pleased to be ___*merciful*___.

Micah 7:20 - You will keep your ___*word*___ and be ___*faithful.*___.

SESSION 20

MICAH: DO JUSTICE, BE MERCIFUL, HUMBLY OBEY GOD

HOMEWORK

Name_____

Reflection Questions

Directions: Review your notes and Activity worksheet from this session to help you best answer the questions below.

1. As the prosecuting attorney for the Lord, Micah begins his case against the people of Israel by reminding them of all the good things God has done for them because of God's steadfast love for them.

    a. Think of all the good things God has done for you and list at least 10 of them below.

    1.
    2.
    3.
    4.
    5.
    6.
    7.
    8.
    9.
    10.

    b. What will you give back to God in return for all that God has done for you? Explain.

© 2001 by Father Flanagan's Boys' Home.

JOURNEY OF HOPE

SESSION 20 HOMEWORK – PAGE 2

2. Micah points out how the sins of the people of Israel have shown their neglect of God, their lack of response to the Lord, and how they betrayed His covenant.

   a. How and why have you been neglecting God?

   b. How have you failed to respond to God?

   c. God's covenant states, "I will be your God and you will be My people." How have you failed to act as one of God's own people?

SESSION 20 HOMEWORK – PAGE 3

3. Micah explains that God requires of us three things - to do justice, to love kindness, and to walk humbly with God.

   a. List five examples of how you could do justice (be fair, do what is right)?

       1.

       2.

       3.

       4.

       5.

   b. List five examples of how you could be merciful (forgiving) in your daily life.

       1.

       2.

       3.

       4.

       5.

   c. List five examples of how you could "humbly obey God" in your daily life.

       1.

       2.

       3.

       4.

       5.

JOURNEY OF HOPE

SESSION 21

Joel: Repent, Restore, Reveal

OBJECTIVE

Enable students to discover and apply to their own lives the prophetic message of Joel.

PREPARATION

Hang three blank poster boards around the room. Entitle one "Repent," one "Restore," and the third "Reveal." Place markers near each poster board.

READER

Chapter 21: Hope and Healing

LESSON PLAN

PRAYER

Opening prayer

REVIEW

Discuss students' responses to the Reflection Questions worksheet from the previous session.

OBJECTIVE

Explain: *"In today's session we'll read and discuss another Old Testament prophet, Joel. The goal of today's session is to help you identify Joel's one-item agenda (prophetic message) and enable you to apply his message to your own life."*

ACTIVITY

Point out the three posters hanging around the room, entitled "Repent," "Restore," and "Reveal." Explain that Joel's one-item agenda is summed up with these three words and that in order to best understand Joel's prophetic message, we need to understand these three words.

1. Ask for three volunteers – one to write on each poster board.

2. Begin at the "Repent" poster. Ask the volunteer to record on the poster board what the class names as synonyms or descriptions of the word "Repent."

3. After creating a list of synonyms and descriptions of "Repent," do the same for "Restore," and then for "Reveal." Spend only 3-5 minutes creating each list.

4. Be sure to add these synonyms and descriptions to each list if not already named by the students:

   Repent – Turn away from evil and go toward good.

   Turn around and go toward God.

   Change from bad to good behavior.

   Restore – Give back what was lost or taken away.

   Bring back to normal condition.

   Rebuild, repair, renew.

   Reveal – Make known what was secret, hidden, unseen.

   See and understand what was previously unknown.

   Show, display, expose to view.

CONNECTION

Have students take the following notes:

- Joel's one-item agenda can be summed up in three words: Repent, Restore, Reveal.

- Joel's message teaches us that:

  1. All people need to repent of their sins and return to living God's ways. (The Ten Commandments)

  2. Through repentance, our relationship with God is restored and renewed and our spiritual selves

become healthier and stronger. We experience God's grace at work in our lives – rebuilding, repairing, and reshaping us.

3. When our relationship with God is restored we will be able to "see with the eyes of faith." God will reveal Himself to us. We will be able to understand and experience God in new and deeper ways.

REFLECTION/HOMEWORK

Distribute the Reflection Questions worksheet. Instruct students to read the book of Joel and answer the worksheet questions. This may need to be completed as a homework assignment. If completed in class, have students read Chapter 21 in the *Journey of Hope Reader*.

SESSION 21 — JOEL: REPENT, RESTORE, REVEAL
ACTIVITY WORKSHEET

Name_____

Reflection Questions

Directions: Read the book of Joel and review your notes on the session. Then answer the following questions.

1. Find three passages from Joel that speak of Repentance. List below the specific chapter, verse, and text that refer to repentance. (Example: Joel 1:13- Put on sackcloth and weep.)

   a.

   b.

   c.

2. Find two passages from Joel that speak of Restoration. List below the specific chapter, verse, and text that refer to God's restoration of His people.

   a.

   b.

3. Find two passages from Joel that speak of Revelation. List below the specific chapter, verse, and text that refer to God revealing Himself and people recognizing God for who He is.

   a.

   b.

4. Read Joel 2:27-29 and answer the following questions:

   a. Verse 28 says, "Later I will give My Spirit to everyone." What do we need to do to receive the Spirit of God?

© 2001 by Father Flanagan's Boys' Home.

JOURNEY OF HOPE

SESSION 21 ACTIVITY WORKSHEET – PAGE 2

    b. Once the Spirit of God is given to everyone, what will we be able to do? (verse 28)

    Sons and daughters will _____

    Old people will _____

    Young men will _____

5. The prophet Joel tells us that if we are to receive God's Spirit, then we must first repent. What sins do you need to repent of? How will you show your repentance?

SESSION 21 ACTIVITY WORKSHEET – PAGE 3

6. Once we have repented, God will restore us to spiritual health through the gift of grace. What specific areas of your spiritual life need strengthening and restoration from God? Explain.

7. Once God has restored us to right relationship with Him and has renewed and strengthened us spiritually through His grace, then God will reveal Himself to us. What about Him do you hope God reveals to you? What has God already revealed to you? Explain.

SESSION 21 — JOEL: REPENT, RESTORE, REVEAL
TEACHER'S COPY

ACTIVITY WORKSHEET

Reflection Questions

Directions: Read the book of Joel and review your notes on the session. Then answer the following questions.

1. Find three passages from Joel that speak of Repentance. List below the specific chapter, verse, and text that refer to repentance. (Example: Joel 1:13- Put on sackcloth and weep.)

 a. *Joel 1:13-14*

 b. *Joel 2:12-13*

 c. *Joel 2:15-17*

2. Find two passages from Joel that speak of Restoration. List below the specific chapter, verse, and text that refer to God's restoration of His people.

 a. *Joel 2:26-27*

 b. *Joel 2:19*

3. Find two passages from Joel that speak of Revelation. List below the specific chapter, verse, and text that refer to God revealing Himself and people recognizing God for who He is.

 a. *Joel 2:28-29*

 b. *Joel 2:30-31*

4. Read Joel 2:27-29 and answer the following questions:

 a. Verse 28 says, "Later I will give My Spirit to everyone." What do we need to do to receive the Spirit of God?

 Repent

SESSION 21 ACTIVITY WORKSHEET – PAGE 2 **TEACHER'S COPY**

    b. Once the Spirit of God is given to everyone, what will we be able to do? (verse 28)

       Sons and daughters will ____*prophesy*_____

       Old people will ____*have dreams*_____

       Young men will ____*see visions*_____

5. The prophet Joel tells us that if we are to receive God's Spirit, then we must first repent. What sins do you need to repent of? How will you show your repentance?

Open-ended

SESSION 21 ACTIVITY WORKSHEET – PAGE 3 **TEACHER'S COPY**

6. Once we have repented, God will restore us to spiritual health through the gift of grace. What specific areas of your spiritual life need strengthening and restoration from God? Explain.

Open-ended

7. Once God has restored us to right relationship with Him and has renewed and strengthened us spiritually through His grace, then God will reveal Himself to us. What about Him do you hope God reveals to you? What has God already revealed to you? Explain.

Open-ended

JOURNEY OF HOPE

Appendix: Social Skills

How to Disagree Appropriately
1. Look at the person.
2. Use a pleasant voice.
3. Say, *"I understand how you feel."*
4. Tell why you feel differently.
5. Give a reason.
6. Listen to the other person.

How to Accept Criticism
1. Look at the person.
2. Say, *"Okay."*
3. Don't argue.

How to Accept a Compliment
1. Look at the person who is complimenting you.
2. Use a pleasant tone of voice.
3. Thank the person sincerely for the compliment. Say, *"Thanks for noticing"* or *"I appreciate that."*
4. Avoid looking away, mumbling, or denying the compliment.

How to Give a Compliment

1. Look at the person you are complimenting.

2. Speak with a clear, enthusiastic voice.

3. Praise the person's activity or project specifically. Tell him or her exactly what you like about it.

4. Use words such as *"That's great," "Wonderful,"* or *"That was awesome."*

5. Give the other person time to respond to your compliment.

How to Ask for Help

1. Look at the person.

2. Ask the person if he or she has the time to help you (now or later).

3. Clearly describe the problem or what kind of help you need.

4. Thank the person for helping you.

How to Share Personal Experiences

1. Decide if you should share personal experiences with the other person.

2. Notice if that person appears comfortable with what you are telling him or her.

3. Share experiences that are appropriate for that person to know.

4. Prompt the other person if what you told him or her is confidential.

How to Express Empathy and Understanding for Others

1. Listen closely to the other person's feelings.

2. Express empathy by saying, *"I understand..."*

3. Demonstrate concern through words and actions.

4. Reflect back the other person's words by saying, *"It seems like you're saying..."*

5. Offer any help or assistance you can.

How to Follow Instructions
1. Look at the person.
2. Say, *"Okay."*
3. Do what you've been asked.
4. Check back.

How to Apologize
1. Look at the person.
2. Use a serious, sincere voice tone, but don't pout.
3. Begin by saying, *"I want to apologize for..."* or *"I'm sorry for..."*
4. Show that you understand by saying, *"Okay," "Thanks,"* or *"I see."*

How to Accept an Apology
1. Look at the person who is apologizing.
2. Listen to what he or she is saying.
3. Remain calm. Refrain from any sarcastic statements.
4. Thank the person for the apology. Say, *"Thanks for saying you're sorry,"* or *"That's okay."*

Social skill steps are taken from *Teaching Social Skills to Youth*, Tom Dowd and Jeff Tierney, Boys Town Press, 1992.

Credits

Production: Mary Steiner
Layout: Anne Hughes
Cover Design: Margie Brabec

009-19-0033